The God
I Know

To Ekanem Frumpong
with highest regards
from the Author.

Victoria Udo

The God I Know

Amazing Supernatural Encounters with Jesus

Victoria Udo

Foreword by Dr. Mark Staller

XULON PRESS

Xulon Press
2301 Lucien Way #415
Maitland, FL 32751
407.339.4217
www.xulonpress.com

Xulon
PRESS

Due to the changing nature of the Internet, if there are any web addresses, links, or URLs included in this manuscript, these may have been altered and may no longer be accessible. The views and opinions shared in this book belong solely to the author and do not necessarily reflect those of the publisher. The publisher therefore disclaims responsibility for the views or opinions expressed within the work.

Unless otherwise indicated, Scripture quotations taken from the King James Version (KJV) – *public domain.*

Paperback ISBN-13: 978-1-66281-676-5
eBook ISBN-13: 978-1-6628-2376-3

TABLE OF CONTENTS

FOREWORD

*M*y wife Sylvia and I met Tom and Victoria Udo in the early 1990s when they moved to the Bay Area with their young family. We attended church together in San Francisco. Our families grew close together at this time, and for the past thirty years Tom and Victoria have been co-laborers with us in spreading the gospel of Jesus Christ. When Tom and Victoria moved to Bakersfield around fifteen years ago, they began faithfully attending our Apostolic Faith Church in Tehachapi, California. (Yes, they have driven about two hours every Sunday for the past fifteen years in order to be part of our church family and part of the Apostolic Faith church work in Tehachapi.) I have had the privilege of being Victoria Udo's pastor during this time.

I have told Victoria before, and I would like to tell you now, that Victoria reminds me of the Apostle Paul. Like Paul the Apostle, Victoria Udo is passionate about spreading the gospel of Jesus Christ throughout the world. Victoria is a "world-class" Christian because she has a heart that beats for two continents, for both America and

Africa. She is truly a hyphenated, "African-American" Christian, because she has travelled between continents and across cultures to further Christian education.

Like Paul the Apostle, Victoria is bold. At the end of his letter to the Ephesians, Paul asks that the saints of God pray "...that utterance may be given unto me, that I may open my mouth boldly, to make known the mystery of the gospel...that therein I may speak boldly, as I ought to speak" (Ephesians 2:19,20). I do not know if Victoria ever prayed a similar prayer, but God has certainly given her the ability and opportunity to speak boldly, like Paul.

Part of Victoria's boldness comes, I am sure, from the power of the Holy Ghost. In Acts 4:29, the Apostles prayed that God would grant unto them "...that with all boldness they may speak thy word...." Acts 4:31 tells us that "...when they had prayed, ...they were all filled with the Holy Ghost, and they spake the word of God with boldness." Like the early Apostles, Victoria has come boldly before the throne of grace and has asked God to bless her ministries and her efforts, and God has blessed her with the gift of the Holy Ghost. Victoria has prophesied, has dreamed dreams, and has seen visions through the Spirit of God.

However, Victoria is also bold because that is just who she is. Boldness is part of her personality. God has given her a bold heart to survive and thrive on the difficult life path that He has designed for her. Losing her father in her teen-age years, living through the dangers of the Biafran war, leaving her family and heading off to college by herself—God knew that Victoria would need a bold heart to make it through the challenging events of her younger years.

God also knew that Victoria would need a bold heart to accomplish all the difficult tasks and to endure the many hardships that He would set before her in her adult life.

In II Timothy 2:3, Paul tells Timothy to "...endure hardness, as a good soldier of Jesus Christ." I think of Victoria when I read this verse. Victoria is a woman, and she has many "feminine" qualities. She loves and depends upon and cooks for her husband Tom. She frets over and dearly loves and prays earnestly for her five children. She likes pretty dresses and flowers and the company of women. However, Victoria has the heart of a warrior. She is interested in pulling down strongholds. She is ready to fight for what she believes in and for those she loves. She is ready to rush to the battlefront for the Captain of her salvation, and she has endured hardness as a good soldier of Jesus Christ.

Victoria does not realize how tough she is. She has presented her body as a living sacrifice to God and to her Lord Jesus Christ, and she has just considered it her reasonable service. She has sacrificed financial security, family time, material possessions, and her physical health to be a pioneering Christian educator in both the United States and Nigeria. She has faced hard trials and unexpected setbacks and she has borne them well. She has an amazing ability to recover and heal both physically and spiritually.

In II Corinthians 11:23-28, Paul lists the hardships he endured as a minister of the gospel of Jesus Christ: "Of the Jews five times received I forty stripes save one. Thrice was I beaten with rods, once was I stoned, thrice I suffered shipwreck, etc." If Victoria sat down and wrote up a list of the hardships she has endured, her list would rival Paul's: "Dozen's of times have I crossed the Atlantic ocean. Thrice have I experienced extreme turbulence. Twice have I contracted malaria, once I have suffered a massive stroke, once was I bedridden with Bell's Palsy, etc."

We thank God for the sacrifices that Victoria has made and for the hardships that she has endured, and we celebrate with her and her family the abundant blessings that God has poured out upon her.

Mark Staller
Professor of Communication
Bakersfield College
Bakersfield, CA

Pastor
Apostolic Faith Church
Tehachapi, CA

INTRODUCTION

I have been favored by heaven to have numerous heavenly encounters along my Christian walk. The encounters are precious and teaching opportunities. It will comfort hearts, encourage steadfastness, motivate you to pray more, and confirm to you that all the claims of scripture are true. Jesus has shown up in strategic seasons of my life to lead the way. It is the manifestation of Psalm 23. These precious moments led to my salvation and great deliverance from dangers. Looking back, there is no way I would still be alive till today, and I am turning seventy in a few days. These testimonies are the right of King Jesus. Shout His praise! Significant above all spiritual exercises is the importance of personal routine times with the Master. These times are spent in Bible reading and speaking with Jesus, which we call prayer. It is also important to read the account of how others got to have victory in their walk. The superficial walk of maybe getting saved and depending only on Sunday sermons will not be sufficient for the journey. It is important to get to hear personally from the Lord. Those personal moments come as you seek

His face continually. God by His Holy Spirit examines your heart at the place of prayer and can root out weeds letting you grow more intimate with Him. He can help you cope with difficult people even pastors, in your life. He teaches endurance which will help growth. I have walked through death's valley but He has been there. Wherever He has placed you, be faithful. I tried to keep the Lord as my reference point, knowing there will be judgement at the end of life. The place of prayer can never be emphasized enough. You pray for the world and see God fight for you. Enjoy the reading and be prepared to share your story in any form. The world needs to hear the exploits of Jesus. He is Alive!

In 1997, as I lay there in Downey Memorial Hospital under the excellent care of Dr. Dana, two creatures entered through the door. I looked at them in my seemingly hopeless situation. As a missionary principal in Watts Christian School, I had suffered a massive stroke three days prior, and that was why I was taken there. In my vision that day, I saw the doctor standing there too. The creatures turned to the doctor, and one of them said, "Why is this woman still alive?"

"I didn't do it," said Dr. Dana. "It's that Book." He pointed to my Bible, which lay on my bedside stand.

I give God glory for the fact that I left that hospital fully recovered. This reminded me of an incident eleven years earlier, in my native land of Nigeria. My husband lay dying and called me to his bedside very early that morning. He started speaking his parting words. "Eno, take good care of the children. I am going the way of all men."

I found a strength within me to refute those words. I sent for two of my praying friends, and they responded immediately. After I shared my story with them, we went into action. We went downstairs and began calling on Jesus. We prayed for about three hours, pleading with God for my husband's life. I presented my case before the Lord. I had suffered as a child after my father died. My own children were too young, and I would not be able to care for them alone. I was too young to become a widow, and there was a host of other reasons. My two friends were praying earnestly too. Then, suddenly, as we continued in prayer, a note was written on a beautiful sheet of paper and put before me. "Expect prevailers at 5:00 p.m.," it said. I jumped to my feet. I told my friends we had received an answer. I shared it with them, and we started singing and praising the Lord. You will see in this book that prevailers came, as I was told they would. This is a little taste of the God I know. I went about that day doing my usual chores with joy, expecting prevailers to arrive. I didn't know what form they would take. I didn't know if they would be visible to the physical eyes. I didn't know if they were a company of angels. Up till that time, I'd never heard of prevailers. My excitement was increasing as the time was approaching. You will learn how it happened in the body of the book.

You have been told so much about Africa and how some things happen there that defy explanation. There are many technological feats that have not been recorded yet in Africa, but in the area of supernatural encounters, God, who does not discriminate, has been generous and encouraging. A lot of exploits are done in the supernatural in Africa because many people there cling to Him in desperate faith. Does Scripture not say that those that come to God must believe that He exists and is a rewarder of those who diligently seek Him? I'm a witness to some of those who have sought God diligently. There seems to be a curtain that has hidden many of those encouraging stories from others in the world. However, there is an area where things happen the same way in Africa as in other lands. I'm writing this based on the concept I had from the beginning—that of building a bridge from Africa to other continents of the world.

Some people may have many questions about Africa. How do people live from day to day? Do children actually go to school? Do people gather in churches to worship as in other lands? Do people love their neighbors as the Bible teaches?

This book lifts the curtain, and you'll be able to see into things you've desired to know. You will see that children are born, raised, and loved like in other places. It's the same God, that is why the scarlet thread that runs across the world passes over the hearts of all who have experienced salvation in Jesus's name. God, our fortress, responds to prayers and praise the same way. He cannot change ever, and that makes it so safe to follow Him. Dare to step into His steps and experience the thrill of His faithfulness. These stories are eyewitness accounts that have never before been written. Welcome to the clashes of the natural with the supernatural. Each time, one dominated. Which one could it possibly be? I joined the winning team. There are thousands of accounts of God's miraculous intervention in the daily lives of saints. Many of those testimonies in Africa have not been written. If they were all written, maybe more people would learn to implicitly trust the Almighty God, maker of Heaven and Earth. I personally have been encouraged by many of those testimonies. You will be very encouraged by the time you reach the end of this book. You'll see that God is still the same. I've been amazed at His faithfulness.

This is an ordinary account of God reaching out in mercy. It was in the night. I had been deeply asleep. Each time I've shared some testimony, my friends and family have said. "Why don't you write some of these to encourage people? Some people have never heard this kind of story in the real world." Christianity is a real-life adventure. Whoever heard a message in the night, so scary and direct, about an impending doom? This was helping to accomplish His plan of redemption in my life. The overflowing effect led to my salvation, the salvation of family members, and that of others. This is a love manifestation of the incredible God. The Bible contains many such loving accounts of God reaching out to lost humanity. But some people are passing by without stopping to pay heed to the messages. That was who I was before this great grace reached me. Many things are happening even now to draw men to God. The time is now for all people to find the salvation of God. There will be a day then there will be no more day. We seem to be drawing very close to that crucial day—the day of the Lord.

We read of women who received a blessing of having their dead brought back to life in the Bible (Heb. 11). In this account, I escaped the harm of bullets because God showed up in a jungle forest farm. Oh yes, He still delivers when there is none other to lean on.

It can't be imagined, but God promised me, as I desperately sought Him in prayer for my dying husband, to send prevailers at 5:00 p.m. They arrived at 5:00 p.m. on the dot because God cannot lie. The details will be enunciated later in this book. There are too many fascinating encounters with heaven, which I believe will encourage your faith. There are more than I can fit into this book.

I write these stories to help us remember that God is alive in the lives of mere mortals like you and me.

However, there are stories in this book of times I've almost been confounded. That doesn't affect the fact that God is alive and still on the throne. Some of the things I've experienced can't be explained. But all I ask is that I be led to love Him more and more and speak like Habbakuk in chapter 3—from the heart. We were not promised a life without problems at all. But He promised to be with us through the fire and through the river.

> "Although the fig tree shall not blossom, neither shall fruit be in the vines; the labor of the olive shall fail, and the fields shall yield no meat; the flock shall be cut off from the fold, and there shall be no herd in the stalls: Yet I will rejoice in the Lord, I will joy in the God of my salvation" (Hab. 3:18–19).

Many authors of fiction have drawn inspiration from these contemporary events. There are many things God has done in the lives of Christians around the world that are not known worldwide. These things fall into the realm of the supernatural. People cling more to desperate faith in God in dire circumstances. Thereby, God proves Himself and comes through gloriously. It has been my prayer that Jesus's power in daily living be broadcast across the globe. This will enable more people to come to a saving knowledge of Jesus. He is still the Savior, no matter what men say or what my own difficult experiences say. That is at the heart of this book. The human mind is amazing and can fashion out many interesting inventions. But nothing surpasses the awe that's inspired by the supernatural works of God. I still get lost in the wonders of creation. I hope you can still look in wonder at your surroundings. Then can anyone conjecture how the Maker of this great universe condescends to connect with one human being? That is my story. That is our story. That can be your story. The only purpose is to bring man to a saving knowledge of Himself. Salvation is the greatest miracle that man can experience.

How can God deliver one from a snake bite in one's living room? But He did. My husband and I are witnesses. It was evening. My husband and I were getting ready for a ride through town. I was ready. My husband still needed to put on his shoes. He casually kicked one shoe before putting it on his foot. Out came a snake and crawled away. We were stupefied. When did the snake enter? How did it find its way in there? What if Etekamba had put his foot straight in, as he usually did? The questions are many. But one thing is certain; God delivers us from evil. He delivered my husband. God still delivers His own. That was the only occasion with the snake. No other snake ever came close to our house to scare us in the two years we lived there. There could be suggestions in our native culture that there may have been something diabolical with the snake. Even if that suggestion holds true, it doesn't change the power of God.

He Still Delivers His Children from Hidden Dangers

The Bible tells us, "Our fathers trusted in thee, they trusted, and thou didst deliver them" (Ps. 22:4).

Sometimes not in answer to immediate prayers. It's good to trust in the Lord always. It should be easier to trust Him than to believe the world, but it's not. Trusting God takes faith. I believe in prayers stored in heaven. Let us pray now, while we can. Pray for the nation; pray for children and grandchildren; pray that others may be saved; pray that preachers may preach with boldness. Pray as the Spirit leads you, and pray that God's will be done on Earth as in Heaven.

> "And another angel came and stood at the altar, having a golden censer; and there was given unto him much incense, that he should offer it with the prayers of all saints upon the golden altar which was before the throne" (Rev. 8:3).

There is a confirmation that the prayers of saints—God's people, you and I—are stored in Heaven. That's what this book is about. You will also share in the prayer requests which answers ache our hearts to see. Some particular prayers have not yet manifested their answers, and we are waiting. You may have some unanswered prayers too. But hold on—the end has not yet come. There is great encouragement in seeing one who is going through some affliction with a cheerful spirit. I'm stating this upfront to say that although we've had an exciting journey with the Lord, as you will attest to, there were still seasons of heaviness.

"And thou shalt love the Lord thy God with all thine heart and with all thy soul and with all thy might" (Deut. 6:5).

He demands wholehearted devotion to Him. It's necessary to give our wholehearted allegiance to the Lord. We owe Him this allegiance because He owns us. He made us. He redeemed us. He is expecting us in glory. He will love our company in eternity. When we consider who Jesus is and how He left His throne to come to Earth that man may live, we see that nothing about our stay on Earth is more urgent than loving Him. In my life of trying to know Him and obey Him and love Him, I can look back on how faithful He has been. The dealings He has had with me along life's journey are worth sharing. The things we find depend on the terrain we walk on, but one thing characterizes it: the faithfulness of the Almighty God.

During this season of the plague (Covid-19), we've been left with a lot of time on our hands. We have a call in this book from the Lord to flee the wrath to come. We can never go wrong fleeing from judgment toward the Lord. As we learn in Zechariah 10:1, He wants the body—His people—to be involved. Ask of the Lord rain in the time of the latter rain. There shall be a turnaround. Many people have been hurt by various words the Lord did not send. But we can never go wrong at the place of asking the Lord. When we have preconceived ideas of what we think God is going to say or do, then we can't ask with a single eye. Those who love the Lord must remember how God answered us in days past. We must prostrate ourselves before Him in earnest prayers. This is the time to pray. We can pray over zoom; we can pray over the phone. However we want to, let us pray. Thy will be done on Earth as it is in Heaven.

Elijah's God must answer again, by fire. God did not send Jesus to redeem the tall buildings, not the huge banks, not the fleets of aircraft, but men. No one is going to be delivered by his good works. Even people we have written off are still candidates for salvation before God.

Jesus added, thou shalt love thy neighbor as thyself.

Men's hearts are failing them in this generation. Some people are very lonely. Some are very destitute. If you stretch out a dollar to a poor man, please add the scripture of salvation. Many are dying and are delivered into a Christless grave. He imprinted on my heart the other day that there is nothing we can do to make God bigger. He just wants us to live well and peacefully among ourselves. Why are people killing their fellow humans? God never sent them to do that.

Oh, for a Fresh Visitation

*G*od's purpose in visiting us is to turn docile people into lively people. We can only imagine what a prayerful church can accomplish at this time. Based on my experience, I know that God needs to stir me up to seek His face for His glory again. The kind of Christian literature that I was exposed to at the beginning of my journey inspired me. The Holy Spirit filled my being. Do you remember *The Passion for Souls*, by Oswald Smith, *Why Revival Tarries*, by Leonard Ravenhill, and a host of others? We can all learn from Scripture. "Behold I stand at the door and knock if any man hears my voice, and open the door I will come into him and will sup with him and he with me" (Rev. 3:20).

That we got saved enables us to hear the Master's voice and open the door for Him. We can sup with Him. The important thing is not to wear a church badge but to feed on the Word, accept challenges, and live by the Word day by day. I have avoided talking about denominations here. I'm talking about Jesus. Just sharing my testimonies and looking back, I can see the difference. As we drive about in our cars on well-lit roads, there are missionaries in villages of indigenous peoples helping to translate the scriptures into their dialect. Our country, once a Christian nation, now has more Sunday beachgoers than churchgoers. Some of us in the church now hate others with a passion. That is not representing the God I know. Those who sup with Him often will hear what He wants. As I study and tarry in his presence, the Spirit says things like "Have you forgiven so and so?" I try to wriggle out of my responsibility, saying something like, "She didn't ask for forgiveness." You can probably guess the rest of the dialogue. It's God's Heaven and not yours. You are a forgiven sinner, and you must leave your offering and go in search of your sister. "To the merciful, He will show Himself merciful."

He says, "Be ye holy for I am holy."

The Bible says, "Love not the world, neither the things that are in the world, if any man love the world the love of the Father is not in him For all that is in the world, the lust of the flesh and the lust of the eyes and the pride of life is not of the Father, but is of the world, And the world passes away and the lust thereof, but he that doeth the will of God abideth forever" (1 John 2:15–17).

Upfront, I want to remind you that God is a holy God. We access Him through prayer. This prayer must have two purposes. We pray for ourselves and for others. This is a major truth about the Christian God. After being born again, I was on cloud nine. But after a time, I found some things of the old life trying to creep back to challenge my victory. That was when we would cue up to ask Every visiting preacher on campus, personal questions. Thank God for the few who spoke of consecration and sanctification. I prayed, and God heard my cry. You will see in my story that my salvation experience was real. I have always wanted authenticity. I am saying this because I have found a difference in Christian styles. A sanctified Christian life is peaceful and gracious. There is an exhibition of the wisdom of God, as stated in James 3:17–18. There are Christians who claim to be always right, and no one can counsel them. Do you know what it is to be easily intreated? A lifestyle of holiness breeds peace. This is for our well-being.

The wisdom from above is, first, pure, then peaceable, gentle, and easy to be intreated, full of mercy and good fruits, without partiality, and without hypocrisy. And the fruit of righteousness is sown in peace by them that make peace.

For some people, it takes suffering to get to the point of submitting to God. There are hearts that yearn for God and hearts that are just fine doing whatever. But the path is narrow. It's either all God's show or all man's show. These are days when many of the young who've been born again, quickly become the disciples of showy men. We all need to get back to Scripture. The God of the Bible will meet with every sincere seeker. He will meet our needs according to His will. Share in this song that I wrote years ago:

The Precious Blood of the Lamb

The Precious Blood of the Lamb
Precious cleansing Blood
Were it not for that Blood
I would be lost

Oft in despair
Or should I say
Groping in dark
Aimless and sad
But thanks to God for Calvary
Where Jesus shed His Blood
That whosoever would believe
Eternal life, eternal life receive

Chorus
O precious Blood,
The cleansing fountain
On Calvary, it freely flowed
Tis victory for the church forever
That Blood will never lose its power

The spotless Blood of the Lamb
Powerful spotless Blood
Were it not for the Blood
Sin with its chain
Would take its toll
And men as sheep
Would live and die
Without a hope
But thanks to God for Calvary
Where Jesus shed His Blood
That whosoever would believe
Unshackled be
Unshackled he would be

—Victoria Udo

I wrote this song a long time ago on my knees during a personal time with God, and it stands true throughout time. It's good to be real with ourselves along this journey from toddler to old age. This God is unchanging, and when we live true, He will show Himself true. He can test us. We can have a few thorns to help us stay humble, but God will always be true.

There are a lot of good words from pulpits in this land. There are powerful women who are teaching others that our "love may abound more and more." But God wants more of His people to pray, according to 2 Chronicles 14:7. As we pray, God has the opportunity to talk to our hearts and elicit a response. The backslidden generation would join the Lord's army. Even denominations that were founded on the altars of prayer are moving further and further away from it. We may have all our needs met, but what of the Lord's needs—the salvation of the lost.

What about Paul's statement to Timothy? "I exhort therefore that first of all, supplications, prayers, intercessions, and giving of thanks, be made for all men; For kings and that for all that are in authority that we may lead a quiet and peaceable life in all godliness and honesty. For this is good and acceptable in the sight of God our Savior" (1 Timothy 2:1–3).

If we take this to heart, we would beef up many of our two-minute prayers. Our land would be quieter. I know that the end, with its wars and commotion, is at hand but the body will continue to do her work, being true watchmen on the walls until He returns. There are situations in which men need to prevail in prayer to attract the intervention of God.

We have a lot of experiences that God has guided us through which can encourage, challenge, or comfort others along the Christian pathway. After spending more than fifty years as born-again Christians we, can share with others our day-to-day lives, including the success and failures, joys and sorrows, and above all, the ever-living presence of the Lord. These all confirm the Word of God.

Let me begin with my growing up on another continent and my subsequent conversion experience as a young adult at the university. That, I believe, is entering in by the door. I was a church girl all along, singing in the choir and partaking in communion, but not knowing I needed a personal experience with God. That was necessary to assure me that I had become a child of God.

GROWING UP DAYS

rowing up in the little town of Eket, Nigeria, by the banks of the Atlantic Ocean, was fun. It was more fun than I can describe. We could hear the roaring of the waves from our home. Fish hawkers would carry about fresh fish, like catfish, tilapia, and croaker, in basins on their heads. They went around the streets shouting, "*Edep iyak*" (buy fish.) Mother bought fish any time of the day and very often made the fisherman soup. Crabs and scallops were abundant, depending on the season. Some of the fish were dried or smoked by the women before being sold. Many of us from that part of the world still import those dried fish to this day.

Dad worked in the local Lutheran hospital, and Mom taught in a nearby elementary school. I had many friends my age, and we would go down to the beach to bathe and swim very often, just along the shallow shore. There was an unfortunate incident one day. After a time of compound work in our primary school, the teacher gave us permission to go down to the river for a bath. We children went down. I don't think the teacher accompanied us. That was not the first day we went to the river with a team from the school. As we were swimming and beating the water, singing and talking, one of us—Mary—was swept away by the waves. We didn't notice until much later when we were about to go back. We screamed and shouted to the adults who were around. Expert swimmers dived into the river and searched for her, to no avail. It was a sad evening as we went back to school without her. Her parents and family wept, and we schoolmates wept too. That left an unforgettable mark in my mind. For some time, we avoided the river.

The mouth of the Eket River is an estuary to the Atlantic Ocean. God has spread beauty across all the earth. Some people recognize these unbought resources; some people do not.

I never appreciated the beauty of this natural scenery until I was grown and started traveling intercontinentally. When I was a child, there was a favorite spot in our home where I would sit to watch nature. It was beside a pillar on our verandah. I watched the rising of the sun, the going down of it, and the different colors of birds or butterflies that would suck nectar from mother's roses. This upbringing planted a love for flowers in my heart. I had a very happy childhood. We didn't own a car, and I never missed it. We had love in the home. We would wait for the evenings, when Dad would tell us stories and sing for us. Sundays were particularly joyful. Dad and Mom would sing "It is well with my soul" while everybody would be getting ready for church. We would sing along as much as we could. I learned a lot of those songs, although I never understood their meaning. But they were melodious. I miss those times, but life can't be reversed. Those simple joys of life can't be bought.

Let me open up a little about the way fondness was shown to the young by the adults. It was mostly through the names we were given. I remember four different names given to me within my immediate family. Daddy had a name for me; Mama had a name for me. There was a household name that my siblings called me, and they still do. Victoria was my name at school. Those nuggets of life gave joy. I have started sharing the truth about this with this culture. I see that God, in His Word, did give people victorious names and changed their old ones.

Like many young children, I had questions, which I would ask in my mind: How did we get here? Where does the sun come from? Is it falling into the river in the evening? There were a thousand and one questions in my mind. God knows all men and knows me. Unknown to me, He had a plan to answer those questions someday, as you will see in this book. Our hospital was a mission hospital, and there was a chapel attached to it. We had church and choir practices, and we celebrated Good Friday, Easter, and Christmas. Dad was a veteran of World War II, fighting on the side of Great Britain, an ally of the United States. He was also a lay preacher. He married my mom after the war.

He told us of his trips to Burma, Glasgow, and Jerusalem, and brought back artifacts to show to the family. I was the first-born child and was treated as very precious. Dad told us he had looked forward to having children since his days of singlehood in World War II. He told us stories about foreign lands. All these made me long to see other parts of the world. When airplanes would fly past, I would ask Dad, "How will I be able to go on one of those?" He told me I needed to work hard in school to be able to achieve such things. I stored that in my heart as I grew up. My grade school principal nicknamed me, Aggrey of Africa, for my inquisitiveness and zeal to accomplish tasks.

There were many motivational quotes that I was exposed to in my childhood. One which has lingered in my heart is:

> The heights by great men reached and kept
> Were not attained by sudden flights,
> But they while their companions slept,
> Were toiling upward in the night.

True to what my daddy told me, hard work pays off. I've been on airplanes more than forty times. One brought our family to the United States of America. It may mean nothing to the rich, but when you consider my starting point, you can see the glory of the God I know. That is why my heart agreed with a certain definition of success. It's not measured by what you have done alone but by the obstacles you overcame on the path to your goal.

My world view was different from those of many other children I interacted with. Words meant the world to me. Dad and the mission hospital chaplain talked of Christian values, but I was afraid to ask them the real question that bothered me. What the pastor taught every Sunday was unattainable, and I just concluded no one was meant to practice the teachings wholly.

Sadly, my dad died before I could complete high school, and the family now depended on my mother alone, with occasional support of her parents. The events of the Biafran War the following year did not make things easier on my teenage mind. Questions upon questions mounted day by day. But where would the answers come from?

Daddy's Death and the Struggle

*Y*ou may be encouraged by my struggle and the good hand of the Lord our God upon me, which opened up university education for me. Dad had died a year before the Biafran War started. Life was hard.

God cares. He stood by a widow.

I was in the eleventh grade when Daddy died. There was no paternal uncle with sufficient means to care for us. My maternal uncles were younger and unable to help my mother. My father's family summoned my mother to a meeting. We, the children, were present. My administrative uncle in the larger family began to speak. He pointed out a few men in the extended family. He wanted my mother to choose one of them for a husband. His reasoning was that my mother would receive help in that way. But remember, my mother already had six of us. All those men were village men with no more than a second or third grade education. Although they attended the family church, they were free to practice polygamy. They were all married men. My mother could not accept any of them. How could she? She boldly stood up before the men and refused their counsel. They had said my brother would be taught palm wine tapping. Today he's an engineer and lives in Arizona. My second brother, who is a medical doctor today, would have learned mending bicycle tires in the village.

My mother boldly said, "I will stay single for my children." There was an uproar. They called her names—obstinate woman, headstrong, and more. Those words didn't move her. We left the village and went back to Eket, where they both worked. My maternal grandma and grandpa were alive and were very helpful. Those were terrible customs, and we praise God, who saw our future and helped my mother to take a stand.

It was not easy for her at all, but God gave her initiatives. One day, as I entered the bedroom, I saw her with both hands lifted up praying out loud, "O, God, how will I care for all these children?"

I quickly ran out. My heart was broken. I made up my mind to help my mother by listening to her advice and loving school so I could earn money and be of help. God of eternal goodness heard me and made a way. My mother experienced salvation and served the Lord before she died. Nothing could make me happier. She was a mother among mothers.

The Start of the Biafran War

*O*ne good morning in school, around ten, we were summoned to an assembly for an address by the principal. We gathered with keen, eager ears, because it was not normal to summon us at that hour to an assembly. The principal informed us that there was secession from Nigeria, and we were no longer Nigerians but Biafrans. We cheered and clapped, not understanding the full implications of what we heard. The national anthem of Biafra was a familiar song. We sang with all our hearts. Yes, we had seen the pogrom in the North—the slaughter of Easterners in huge numbers true that Southern Nigeria which included us in the Southeast are Christians. The Northerners are mostly Muslims. We had peacefully coexisted for years. But what happened? I recalled seeing a newspaper account of a woman whose breasts had been cut off. It was a horrible sight. Something in my young heart agreed that secession was the answer.

We were told that school was closing, and many of us were happy to go home and eat home-cooked food. We didn't know that it would be for longer than one, two, or three months. Little did we know that our learned principal, Mr. Obot would be killed. After we were pulled out of school, life was without structure and uncertain. The usual items of food gradually disappeared from the stores. There were bans on this and that. Mom struggled to stand in line, and she would receive powdered milk and a few other things to help us eat. Some of the foods we had never seen before. The Red Cross made these possible. There were times when the bomber planes roared close to distribution centers, and the people in lines fled. The war lasted for years, but we students went back to school the next year.

The style of women's dresses in this part of Africa was a bit tight around the knee at this time. It was called (tight knee). So Mom told us she had to tear her skirt to be able to run in the confusion from the bomb that was dropped. This kind of incident happened often during those war months. Sometimes it was running from a bank line. Money was rationed, though it was our own. That was my experience, being raised by a strong single mom during the Biafran War. In those days, we saw the hand of God caring for us, His creatures. I remember there was an abundance of mushrooms growing in the fields and on the farms surrounding our homes. That was a great source of nourishment for all the families in Southeast Nigeria. The routine was to get up quickly in the mornings and gather mushrooms for food. This helped sustain the population. But for the help of the Lord, I may not have been alive to tell of this great goodness.

"He opens His hand and satisfies the desire of every living creature" (Ps. 145:16).

"The Lord is good to all and His tender mercies are over all His works" (Ps. 145:9).

Mushrooms Like
Manna in the Region

*T*he staple diet of this region consisted of *akara* (made from black eye pea) and *akamu* (porridge from corn) in the mornings, *garri* and soup in the afternoon or evenings, with rice beans, plantain, and varieties of yams. We were blessed with a lot of seafood coming from the Atlantic Ocean. But here came the war, and fishermen were no longer allowed in the seas and rivers. Hunters were restricted too. Rearing cattle and goats almost faded. My grandfather was very careful not to expose his cows but raise them near the house.

There was a stay-at-home order, like during the Covid lockdown. The difference was that the enemy was visible to the naked eye. Children were still being born. People needed to eat, but the choices we had were few. There were families that could not afford more than a meal a day. We had relocated to our native village in Ndiya, with maternal and paternal grandparents. That is where the war met us. It was a blessing that Mom had her parents alive, and they were very helpful and involved in our lives. Their house was a few yards away from the Ndiya River. My eldest maternal uncle was a headmaster, but the war brought him to the village too. Life was a little exciting because we got to hear all the special stories about the progression of the troops. My eldest maternal uncle was in hiding, and his car was hidden, with a lot of leaves on top and around it. Uncle was one of the prominent people and was in hiding. We were not to talk about his whereabouts. What concerned me most was the food. Somehow, all of us of that generation, all across the Southeast of Nigeria, will remember it as the season of mushrooms.

Daily mushrooms were a given. How could God look out for His creation so much? I still ask myself. Where did the mushrooms come from? Where did they disappear to? Could the Lord have answered the prayers of our elders and sent them mushrooms for meat? I will never know the complete answer. My grandparents were remnants of the people who met Samuel Bill, the missionary from England who came up the Qua Iboe River and brought the Qua Iboe mission.

Grandpa's name was Nelson. My mother, Alice, was one of the young women who attended Grace Bill School for Girls, in Eket. The women in the village were fervent in attending women's fellowships. I saw Grandma officiating in women's meetings a lot of the time. They prayed together. They had wrapper uniforms. In short, they did the best they knew how. God looked out for them and their children during the war.

With the mushrooms everywhere, we needed the dough for *fufu* because women could no longer go into distant farms for cassava to produce gari.

We depended on the cocoyam for foo-foo. Little did I know that cocoyam was the richest in nutrients of all the carbohydrates we consumed. I realized that very recently from research. We regarded the people who ate cocoyam as poor people. But because extensive farming of yams could not be done, we depended on the alternative, which could be planted near homes with very little labor. The cocoyam flourished, and we had mushroom soup with cocoyam foo-foo. Salt was scarce and was one of the items the Red Cross would bring to our state. The shops were closed. Life was hard. Many died of kwashiorkor. War is a bad thing. But God preserved my siblings and me. He preserved my uncles, aunties, grandparents, and friends.

I was born in southeast Nigeria, and the war ravished the land. Many young people died of hunger. I will leave that to your imagination. Wartime is a bad time. Keep in mind that most of our high schools were boarding schools. So after the closing of the schools, all the students were home, with no definite agenda. Many of the young men—eighteen years old and above—were conscripted into the military. Youthful exuberance pushed them in, but they were not trained, so many died. The younger boys and the girls remained at home. There were some local markets. The market women told of dead bodies on the roadside.

One day, the war got to my village of Ndiya. My mother did a thing we will never forget. She assembled the six of us. She told us the advancing soldiers were almost here. She split us into two teams, my immediate younger brother, Uko, and I, herself, and the four youngest, Ekpedeme, Uduak, Idaresit, and Albert. She said, "I do this so that if one party gets wiped out, the other party will remain."

She rehearsed our family story to us. Any of you living will be able to tell the family's story. We embraced and said our good-byes. I felt it. Our hearts were heavy. Would I ever get to see my mother again? But we didn't know God was watching over us.

> "Thine eyes did see my substance, yet being imper-
> fect, and in thy book all my members were written,
> which in continuance were fashioned, when as yet
> there was none of them" (Ps. 139:16).

He who made us saw us until this very moment.

My brother Uko was silent, and together we set out for about twelve miles on foot. We were sent to the right, while Mom and my siblings went to the left. The very young ones did not know what grave danger the family was in. I don't know how mother managed with the very young ones. Uko and I crossed the first obstacle, the Ndiya river, on the pontoon bridge. Civilians were not allowed to drive cars at this time. Whenever we heard the sound of a car, we hid in the swamp, because we knew those were soldiers. Maybe my brother and I were given the family's means of transportation, the bicycle.

One day our hostess took me to the farm. I was very scantily clad. Suddenly the bush in front of us appeared to move, like in the account Julius Caesar. Soldiers in camouflage emerged, carrying leaves that made them look like a moving forest. I almost fell to the floor but for a voice that spoke out in my dialect. The voice said, "Begin to jump up and down and show signs of rejoicing. These are soldiers who have come to liberate your people. Shout welcome while retreating. Say you are grateful for their sacrifice. Tell the people to give them coconut and whatever they can lay their hands on."

Remember, these were mostly men and just us two females. Military trucks were just driving slowly beside the battalion. Although they were our countrymen, I had never seen people with tribal marks. The fright was real. I had heard of what soldiers did to young women. This compounded my fears. My lips were literally quaking until we escaped into the nearby houses. Imagine finding yourself in the midst of a forest with these strange men. But I am still alive. I can't go into the horrible experiences we encountered in strange surroundings, but God saw us through, kept us alive.

After this unexpected meeting with the troops, stories started floating around that our village had been burnt down. My brother and I were very sad. For many days, we could find no consolation. One good day, a message came from our mother. We jumped for joy. We were summoned back home. The family was safe. We were reunited with the rest of the family. I remember this with great gratitude. These were two teenagers fleeing for their lives without a guide.

"Thou art a helper of the fatherless" (Ps. 10:14b).

It was after this ordeal that we went back to school. Some of our classmates never returned. Some had died. Students from some other schools who found our school nearer to their homes joined us. Money was scarce. I don't know how my mother managed to send us back to school but she did. I had an academic scholarship before the war. Mothers had to pawn their expensive wrappers. There were soldiers at the checkpoints everywhere, and there were stories of rape and other forms of cruelty. But God kept me safe. There were times I had to disembark a cyclist and dash into the bush to hide. More than once, the soldiers would stop and fire their guns into the bush to scare us and force us to come out. It didn't work on me. I'm alive to tell this story now. I experienced the sacrificial love of my mother and grandparents. Any other version of motherhood is different for many of us who came from this background. After the liberation of our town and nearby cities, we went back and finished high school.

> "For I know the thoughts that I think toward you,
> saith the Lord, thoughts of peace and not of evil, to
> give you an expected end" (Jer. 29:11).

Through all the dangerous times of life, God preserved me for His purpose.

I never thought of going to the university initially. After Dad died, I thought that meant the end of my dreams. But God has plans for us we can't always see. Here the Lord's compassion broke through. After passing with division one in my school certificate exam, Mother took us from Eket to Calabar to live with a family

An Open Door

I had never met. It was a bittersweet existence. I remember always walking more than two miles to the market to buy food stuff, while the children of the home went to school. I endured all in hope that someday I would find freedom by finding a job and renting my place.

One morning, as I was sweeping the living room, the man of the house came out of his room as an announcement came over the radio. It said there was an entrance examination into the University of Ife and that interested applicants should come for the exam. Immediately the owner of the house spoke. I saw the intersection of destiny and opportunity. He said, "Vicky, your mother brags about your intelligence. Stop sweeping and let Raphael, the driver, take you to the exam on Calabar road."

Remember, no one ever prepared me for this exam. I didn't know what area to answer questions in. But I remembered a conversation with my late father, helped me. I opened the science section and decided to answer questions in science. I remember one of those questions today. The question was, "All flesh is grass. Explain." I continued just answering questions until the time was over. I went back home and forgot all about the exam. I didn't know how to find out the result, nor did I dwell on it. The Biafran War was still going on in other parts of the country. In the meantime, I secured a job as a clerk and was earning money. It was seventeen pounds ten shillings per month. I proudly took all the first month's salary to my mother. That pleased me very much, and Mom was happy too. At last, I was going to be able to help her with taking care of my siblings. She gave back some of the money to me.

Just two months after the entrance exam, my attention was drawn to an item in the newspaper. My name appeared with others as having passed the exam. I was admitted to the University of Ife to study for a BS in chemistry. Now the school is called Obafemi Awolowo University. I was overjoyed and ran to tell my guardian about my admission.

He poured cold water on my head. "Do you think everybody is meant to attend a university?" he said. "Do you know people pay to go to school?"

This comment sparked something inside me. I was ready to fight for my future. The man invited my mother and my uncles to Calabar for a meeting. At the meeting, my boss, who had a PhD from an American university, put fear in my family to discourage me from thinking about university education. So many reasons were promulgated. But I found courage within my heart to defy all those elders, announcing that I was bent on going to the university. But they knew that between me and that goal was funding.

My mother was emotional. She left her seat and came to hold me, pleading with me to listen to her and the assembly. I told her that my obstinacy was in her favor, because if I didn't find a way to higher education, then my siblings would have no motivation to go forward in education. That meant that even children who lacked our kind of brain power would go beyond us in life. Eventually, they would employ us. And all that would happen just because Dad had died.

I wept, and the meeting broke up. I assured my mother that my obstinacy was for the good of our family. I had seen her fight so hard, with little money to use for our education. She baked bread to sell. She made soap for our use and for sale. She always had a kiosk for selling little household items.

God is a God of the widows and the fatherless. "The Lord preserveth the strangers; He relieveth the fatherless and widow" (Ps. 146:9).

After leaving that oppressive assembly of friends and foes, I kept making up different scenarios in my heart. I may have called on God. I'm not sure. But whatever the case, the merciful God of heaven was looking out for me. I felt some inner strength. I knew that my having a university education would be a blessing to our family. At that time, only a few privileged ones were beneficiaries. It looked very unattainable.

An idea came up in my heart. I drafted a letter that told my story, and I took it around to kind families that knew my dad. It took about a week. They donated money to me. It was enough for my airfare to Lagos and more than a term's school fees. I showed the money to my guardian, and he took out some for my transportation. He said he was sending the rest, fifty-six pounds, to his friend, a professor at Ife University, to hold for my fees. I had a little for pocket money.

I had five dresses made for me, and on the appointed day, I was off by air to Lagos, on my way to the university. You may have a laugh at some of my inexperience. I had never traveled in an airplane. I had never left the Southeast. I never thought of how I would find the person who was to pick me up. My guardian had told me some name of a person who would pick me up at the airport.

Only God knows if he actually did contact anybody to do that. I say this because the money he took from me never arrived at the university, even by May, when exams were about to begin. But when God sets out to bless you, no man can stop Him. He is the omnipotent. What a Savior!

There was nobody with a sign to pick me at the airport. The flight was empty and ready for another take-off, but there was no one in sight for me. Then my mind went to work. God must have been looking out for this fatherless girl. I saw a policewoman with a name tag that read, Efik/Ibibio by origin. I summoned courage and approached her. I narrated my story, and she immediately took me with her to her car. This is a typical Efik/Ibibio characteristic. We are hospitable and accommodating. God placed her there for me, I believe. On getting home, she fed me dinner and gave me a warm place to sleep. The next morning, she made me prepare promptly and sent her driver to drop me off at Ife Motor Park. I paid into the back of a pickup truck. There were women with all sorts of wares to sell. They were speaking very loudly in their language, but I was too excited to be bothered. "I am going to university." I said. "Oh, what joy!"

OFF TO COLLEGE

$\mathcal{N}$ ow I found myself at the University of Ife, surrounded by breathtaking beauty. There were lush fields, assorted flowers lining the paths, and thick patches of green foliage never tampered with by man. The mile-long driveway into the campus was planted with the most breathtakingly beautiful flowers of orange, purple, yellow-white, and all. It was an outstandingly beautiful university, with modern architecture. It was acclaimed as the second largest university in the world on one site (nine square miles, not completely developed yet). Professors from Europe, America, and Asia joined their Nigerian counterparts to provide quality education. The campus sat amid healthy green vegetation, away from the rumbles of the city.

My one focus was to focus. I just wanted to do my school work, graduate on time, and go back home. After all, Mom, a widow, was toiling alone with the other five children. She had no assistance.

As I mentioned, the money I'd struggled to raise had never arrived. It was not sent. I kept telling the school authorities that money was coming. At one point, my mattress was folded up, and I was evicted from the dorm. I still managed to take my baths and use the restroom. The hall porters were given my name, and they could sneak in for a check anytime. This was stressful, to say the least. But I was resolved to stay.

There were days I waited until the boys had finished playing draft in the common room. I would then put two of the tables together and spread a mat under them to sleep. Angels were watching over me. No harm ever came to me. I would wake up by five to go have a shower, before others came. But this is the God I know, who helped me in my lowly state. That is why I shout my praise and cannot be silent. I struggled and passed my final exams that first year. I was still a nominal Christian.

During the very first long vacation, everybody parked outside waiting for their rides. My mother didn't know where this her daughter was I waited too but for nobody because I was three hundred miles from home. As I stood under the shade of a tree, I started a conversation with one of the students. I got to know that the police officer in charge of the adjacent campus was from the Southeast. As we stood, the officer came around, and behold, it was Emem's dad. I was friends with his daughter in Lutheran high school. He was overjoyed to see me.

I asked about my friend and learned she was home. So God, in His sovereignty, had kept a family to watch over me. I can't go into the details of care. I was a daughter. This first year passed, and I didn't find the fellowship girls. The newspaper that showed my result for this first year was always with me when we went down to Lagos to their home.

There I went to look for a job. Some people pointed to the Imarsel Chemical Company. I boldly went in there to ask whether there was any vacation job. The managing director was a sober-looking man, very dignified and of a class. He looked at me, and I stood there looking like a high school student.

He spoke very officially to me. "Can you show proof that you are a university student and that you passed your examination?"

I quickly brought out the folded newspaper and proudly showed him my name. He rang the bell for his secretary. He immediately dictated a letter for the university. He said the company has taken over my schooling to pay the fees. He also arranged a sum of money for my books. He got fifty pounds from his cashier and handed it to me with the instruction that I was to buy clothes and dress like an undergraduate.

I was beside myself because it was more than I requested. Yet it was what I needed. I feel I'm reliving that experience as I write. I was also given a vacation job. That put me on cloud nine, and I went back to my host family to tell my story. I humbly recount these mercies because this shows the nature of God Almighty, to show mercy.

"That ye may be the children of your Father which is
in heaven: for he maketh his sun to rise on the evil
and on the good, and sendeth rain on the just and
on the unjust" (Matt. 5:45, KJV).

I was now a company scholar when the new session began. We now moved to the new campus of the university. I had joined the sports team. I played netball for the university. One day, I was coming back from one of those games on a train. The news came over the speaker that Mr. Etim, the owner of Imarsel Chemical Company, had died. As he was showing a foreign partner around his shipyard, a crane fell on him and crushed him. Why did this happen? This is the man who showed me and other students mercy. What was I going to do with my education? It was a sad trip from Jos to Ife. I traveled with a very heavy heart.

Within a few weeks, I received a letter saying that the company would no longer pay my school fees. I traveled from IleIfe for his burial. No one knew me there, but I was one of the saddest people at the funeral. Did I need to go there, traveling all those miles, on a bad road? Yes. I never saw that man more than once, but his kindness left an imprint on my heart. May I return that kindness to some person in need? See how far He has brought me. He is Jehovah Jireh, the Provider.

Things were about to open up concerning my quest after God, as I studied in the university. Answers to questions I had wrestled with were about to unfold when I was no longer asking. I had long ago resolved to just live like every other person.

On this campus, I could only say, wow! Wow, what beauty! What challenges! What a mix the world had. The circumstances of survival in my early days on campus would take another book to tell. But it was at the university that real answers started coming, not from the professors, but from God. Oh yes, I had world-renowned professors who taught us well in the various academic disciplines. Many of the graduates of this university have gone on to great exploits in the world. The truth is that many perplexities of life are not explained in the classrooms. There is the spiritual part of man that will live forever. It is this spiritual part that directs man on this planet, consciously or unconsciously. This is the part that must be made alive so that man can find his way.

I left the university with more than a science degree. My eyes were opened, and my life questions were answered. Many, reading this book, have eyes that have been opened. It's eternal joy, no matter the obstacles along the path. But you know that with time people become complacent. That's a dangerous place to be. To the few who have not yet found this open door, your eyes may get opened if you keep an open heart as you read on.

God Broke through the Ceiling

No sooner did classes commence on the new campus than some undergraduates took it upon themselves to give me Gospel tracts. I hated this with all my heart. What suggested that I was a pagan and needed to be converted? I had grown up in a family where the Bible was read, and church attendance was not optional. I dare say that we need guidance in spiritual matters, but at that time, I thought I didn't need anything more. But these friends started praying in their small groups for me, as I later learned. They had prayed for about four months, then an opportunity emerged. There was a Christian outreach weekend on that university campus, and God broke the ceiling to get to my heart. Prayers of the redeemed are powerful. I am so glad people prayed and prevailed.

A Message from Heaven

It was on the night of Friday, January 15, 1971, that this happened to me. It was life-changing, the greatest event of my entire life. It was motivated by love, though it was frightening. I had never heard the like of it before. I speak about it with such reverence for my Creator God. Who else could have done such a great life-changing thing? None but the Lord. I still feel blessed, favored, noticed, and helped greatly. This is how it happened.

Suddenly, at about three in the morning, I saw a scene as if I were watching a video. A very beautiful greeting card was given to me. I wondered at its beauty and peculiarity. On the front was beautiful image of extremely fresh green grass, nicely mowed. There was a herd of sheep walking on it toward a dome-like gate. The sheep were walking in a very orderly way toward this entrance. I was lost in its beauty and wonder. So many questions bombarded my mind. For what occasion was this card sent to me? Animals can't be walking on a card. Then, excitedly, I opened the card. I was shocked and dazed by these words: "**There is an impending doom**, and you have been warned to flee, and you have been promised the spirit."

These words were twinkling like diamonds. Wow! I tried to wrap my mind around it but couldn't make sense of the message. I tried to understand it for some time. Then it occurred to me to check and see who had sent this message. I turned the card over and saw, where the signature should have been, the words "From the Temple." I knew immediately that this message was not from Earth. It must be from Heaven.

"And I saw no temple therein for the Lord God Almighty and the Lamb are the Temple of it" (Rev. 21:22).

I saw this in the Word many years later, and it affirmed that the almighty, in His mercy, sent those gracious words to me, a sinner.

I woke up screaming. My roommate, Grace, a part three law student, reprimanded me for being so loud and waking her up. I apologized and told her nobody who saw such dazzling scenery could do anything differently, and she went back to sleep. The three hours before dawn were the longest hours of waiting in my life up to then. Since then, I have found some long hours (like waiting for the births of my children). Finally, it was six in the morning, and I went straight to Room 95, where prayers had been going up from day to day in Moremi Hall.

Let me take you into our women's hall before proceeding. I lived on the first floor of Block Four in Room 93. Two doors down from me were two girls, Mojisola and Christie. Many times while passing their door, I could hear them praying. I thought of why they needed to pray so much and concluded that they must have come from some idol-worshipping homes. But I found out that I was wrong. They were always having a time of fellowship with the Lord and praying for the students to be saved. Mojisola (Moji, as I called her) and Christie lived here, if I remember. God has the record.

So on this very important day, I knew where to go and to find answers for my perplexity. I asked Moji and Christie if they would have any Christian meeting that day. It was now my turn to search out where Christian meetings were held. All of this because God had singled me out to help. The race had started. I was beginning to flee. The young lady graciously told me about their ongoing meetings and invited me to one that day. Does that not show a God who orchestrates well for human beings? I was told they were going to hear a guest speaker a little ways off. By eight in the morning, the van had come to the porter's lodge, and it took us to yet another beautiful campus. I took my Bible and wore the most decent dress I had, for these were the days of miniskirts.

God had broken through my resolute will. I knew I needed more of God. I needed the real thing and not the counterfeit. Enough of nominal Christianity. I had made up my mind I needed to find God and escape the impending doom. There was singing in the bus, and once in a while, I would sing a loud note to draw some attention to myself. This poor flesh was struggling for some recognition. The flesh was going to die so that Victoria would begin to live victoriously. What a Savior! Everything happening on the bus meant nothing, for my heart was racing with questions. We finally arrived at the venue of the meeting, and events of the outreach commenced.

At the meeting, there was quite a lot of singing and preaching and the chatter of friends, but I was pensive. I don't remember what the preaching was about, sad to say. One thing was sure. God had sent a startling message to me, and I was not going to joke with my chance. The girls sang about all the things young people do in the name of enjoyment that the Bible calls sins. I debated within myself and wondered if those singers were free from all those things. Then there was an intermission. We all went outside. I found a private place to sit on the green lawn, and I brought out my journal and began making notes. There was a direction for me now. What were the things in my life that would hinder me from finding God and submitting to Him? I asked. I made a list of things I considered important that might hinder me:

> Father—none
> Mother—but she won't hinder me
> Money—I don't have
> Friends—Possibly, but I can also make new ones
> Boyfriend—He can't restrain me, or we call it quits

This was my paltry list. Nobody there knew what I was doing. It might be a little costly, I thought. Nothing of eternal value was on this list I had made. I mused.

I didn't see anything that could prevent me from making my own decision and fleeing from the impending doom. I started feeling happy because my heart was turning to Jesus. I made a resolution that if ever a woman loved God with everything, that I would also. We went back inside and continued the meeting. I had started conversing with the good God of Heaven.

It was time to get back to the campus dorm. My mind had been made up that I was going to practice my brand of Christianity. I was not going along with the fellowship girls who did not dress attractively and tied their scarves a lot of the time. But God's eyes were still on me. As soon as we arrived at the dorm, all my girlfriends who had not seen me all day swooped down on me. My boyfriend was at the University of Lagos. Some of the girls said, "Oh you went with the new lifers, so you won't need this item and that item anymore." They raided my room for my makeup. There was a little moment of self-pity after they left me. I summed up courage and continued to face my life that night, I prayed and slept. I had questions about the future. But God does not do things halfway. He had not finished with me.

I had to plot my physics graphs before going to bed. In the morning, there was yet another God moment. It was God's love for me displayed beautifully. After deciding I was not going to church that morning, so I could catch up on all my work, something happened. There was beautiful singing coming from upstairs. It was not easy to resist. So I climbed to the third storey and looked into the common room the music flowed from.

"Come in, come in," said a kind voice. King Jesus had finally led me to a place of total surrender. I sat in with them. Some of the faces I had seen the day before, at the special meeting off-campus. They continued their meeting. At this point, people were testifying of how they had yielded their hearts to Jesus as Lord and Savior. After listening to a few testimonies, I could no longer keep quiet. I jumped up from my seat and asked everyone to stop talking and pray with me to have my own experience and testimony too. Heaven came down. They cooperated and got on their knees with me for a good prayer time. The order of events was not as important as a soul returning to the Savior.

There was earnest praying in the room. I was on my knees seeking God earnestly, asking that He may assure me of my salvation. I can't say how long that prayer time took. But I certainly know I missed lunch that afternoon. It didn't matter that I would miss my chicken, rice, and ice cream. Nothing compared to the fact that I had overflowing joy and peace when I got up from my knees. There were hugs and hugs. I remember walking down the corridors, and everything appearing so small. I felt like floating on top of the world. What a Savior! Finally, my sins had been washed through faith in the blood Jesus shed on Calvary's cross for all mankind. I had entered by faith into my share of redemption. The cleansing stream still flows. God does not complicate the salvation message. That was the message John the Baptist preached. He asked the crowd who had warned them to flee. You flee from the wrath of God through repentance.

There are many practical steps involved in fleeing from an impending doom. You may need to change friends. You may need to change tastes and desires. You need to change loyalty and cling to the God of heaven. In the light of eternity and the individual, one definitely must begin living by the sacred book, the Bible. It's not easy to start living by the Bible, but the Spirit gives help. If you're reading this page now, it's the help of the Spirit that led you here. It's the love of God that brings about such an opportunity. To look back at how heaven opened over my head is a frightening event. But I'm grateful for such a letter from the God of heaven. One does not hear of such matters often. I am grateful. I am grateful. I'm forever grateful. It doesn't happen like this every day for every person. But God wants us to share.

A new day had dawned for me. Was I about to get answers to questions my mind had tossed about since childhood? So there is a God who is keenly interested in mere mortals? That means the Bible is true, and God can enable man to walk in His counsel with the help of His Spirit. He reveals Himself to whomever He chooses. How blessed was my family! Everyone would come to know that there is a God who is very near and who loves humanity very much. He had broken through the ceiling of my heart and had spoken to me. He had washed away all my sins and I felt clean. I now had a testimony. By the time I graduated from this university, I'd have more than a paper degree from a group of men. I would have a testimonial from the God of the universe that I was saved by the blood of Jesus Christ. No one who's had this experience would want to exchange it for a trillion dollars. This puts humans in a separate category called the sons of God. The change that occurs is miraculous. All who have been redeemed are described thus: "And such were some of you: but ye are washed, but ye are sanctified, but ye are justified in the name of the Lord Jesus, and by the Spirit of our God" (1 Cor. 6:11).

This is the summary of the transaction. I had always known that I was a sinner. I had thought that if my good deeds were more than the bad deeds, then God would take me to Heaven. So I tried working my way through church attendance, singing in the choir, doing various kind deeds, but it did not make my heart new. I now acknowledged that I was a sinner, whom Jesus died for. I confessed my sins according to the scriptures, forsook them in my heart by faith, and turned away. By faith, I believed that Jesus died for my sins, and I invited Him to come and be Lord of my life. He answered that prayer and came into my heart.

"Behold I stand at the door and knock, if any man hears my voice and opens the door, I will come into him and sup with him and he with me" (Rev. 3:20).

I was converted and became a born-again Christian. I now have a testimony, like all other born-again Christians. This is called the new birth. Many Christians explain it in different ways, but the effect is the same. When one is born again, it becomes natural to do right. This new life has affected whole cultures, like in the days of preachers like Jonathan Edwards, who wrote the sermon "Sinners in the Hands of an Angry God." The Methodist brothers, John and Charles Wesley, were the first to teach on sanctification. They preached the simple Gospel of Jesus Christ, and England was changed. I read that their mother, Susannah Wesley, prayed prevailing prayers. This Gospel inspired many to do many noble deeds in days gone by.

It is a historical fact that Mary Slessor left a beautiful home in England and came to the jungles of Africa to save twin babies and their mothers. I asked what the big deal was about twin babies. I was told that our cultural blindness said children born as twins were evil. They were not allowed to live. But Mary Slessor, with the power of the Holy Spirit, explained that there was nothing wrong and that twin babies and their mothers should be allowed to live. She went into the jungle to free up abandoned and tied up mothers and their children. May I inform my readers that Africa is no longer a jungle, as many have thought? Civilization marches on. Her grave is with us in Calabar, Nigeria, in Africa, till today. In essence, the gospel of Jesus is a life-changing power wherever it is preached. When He breaks through to you, you can never be the same. That is when good works make sense.

Saying that God broke through the ceiling is my way of describing my conversion experience. God of the universe is not partial. What He does for one person, He can do for all who care to ask. Paul had an experience, and he wrote to the Ephesians about it. "How that by revelation he made known unto me the mystery; (as I wrote afore in few words, Whereby, when ye read, ye may understand my knowledge in the mystery of Christ). Which in other ages was not made known unto the sons of men, as it is now revealed unto his holy apostles and prophets by the Spirit; That the Gentiles should be fellow heirs, and of the same body, and partakers of his promise in Christ by the gospel" (Eph. 3:3–6, KJV).

We are fellow heirs with the people of God. The door of mercy has been opened to all mankind. It is the most awesome privilege.

Prayer is the key to obtaining seemingly impossible things. It was in answer to the prevailing prayers of God's people that God reached out to me. God just does as God wants and consults no one. Our prayers are for the unsaved at this time, especially my generation of believers. We can form a huge resource for our God through our prayers. The saints before us prayed.

Follow-up was a vital part of this campus fellowship group.

Beautiful memories linger in my mind of things that happened there more than fifty years ago. Saints are not only in heaven; they are here on earth too. Jesus makes sinners become saints. No sooner had I become converted than one of the more mature believers took it upon herself to disciple me. The Lord helped me to submit to her guidance. It's called follow-up. There was no idea that I could do my thing myself. Yeti came very early in the mornings to read the Bible with me. It was more than reading; it was a study. This study helped me walk carefully with the Lord. This was the pattern. We started with the Gospel of John daily in this manner:

1) Have a devotional book and my Bible and a notepad.
2) Kneel by the bed with Yeti (she was a final year chemistry student).
3) Use some well-thought-out questions to examine the scriptures, and then pray. (courtesy of the Scripture Union)
4) Examples of the Questions are, what does this passage teach me about
   a) God the Father, b) God the Son, c) the Holy Spirit?
5) Is there any good example for me to follow? Is there any bad example for me to avoid?
6) What prayer can I pray in line with this scripture?

This was such a close fellowship. Our first passage was from John.

> "In the beginning, was the Word, and the Word was with God, and the Word was God. The same was in the beginning with God. All things were made by him, and without him was not anything made that was made. In him was life and the life was the light of men. And the light shineth in darkness; and the

darkness comprehended it not. There was a man sent from God, whose name was John. The same came for a witness, to bear witness of the Light, that all men through him might believe. He was not that Light, but was sent to bear witness of that Light. That was the true Light, which lighteth every man that cometh into the world. He was in the world, and the world was made by him, and the world knew him not. He came unto his own, and his own received him not. But as many as received him, to them gave he power to become the sons of God, even to them that believe on his name: Which were born, not of blood, nor of the will of the flesh, nor of the will of man, but of God. And the Word was made flesh, and dwelt among us, (and we beheld his glory, the glory as of the only begotten of the Father,) full of grace and truth" (John 1:1–14).

Could it be that I was understanding the Word for the first time in my life?

Unbelievable, something true, real, and authentic had happened to me. In a flash, I began enjoying the scriptures. God indeed had broken through to my heart. Whoever has had this experience can understand. There was excitement in my soul. But we must keep this habit of being in God's Word until we depart for eternity. The Word is a lamp. Here are the kinds of questions we used. These questions have helped countless Christians.

Let me share the first digest of the scripture we used to analyze the word for daily living:

Question 1: What is this passage teaching me about God?

Answer: It is that He (God) was in the beginning and the Word, who is Jesus, was also in the beginning. So my eyes were opening to eternal truths. What joy, what hope, what confidence. God is the Creator. The world did not just come to be. This world has a Creator. He is the landlord of the universe and the whole earth.

Jesus is the light of the world, and darkness cannot overcome this light. A little flame of light illuminates a great length of darkness. He saves us, and we become light sources in a dark world. What a privilege. I am screaming as I write.

Question 2: What good example is there for me to follow?

Answer: A good example for me to follow is that, like John, who was sent to be a witness for Jesus, I am also a witness.

Can you sense my joy yet? Nothing else in the whole wide world mattered as much as this. Do you have this joy unspeakable? You can also be a witness if you're not one already. This Lord did the unimaginable for humanity. Can He get a witness? The inspiration went far. I shared my conversion story with anyone willing to hear me. I still share. I never waited to be prompted, but the Holy Spirit does the prompting. Writing this book is still sharing the message of divine love. I believe you have a story too.

Question 3: What was a bad example to avoid?

Answer: I avoid refusing Jesus, as some did in His day. Many did not receive Him then. Many today refuse to accept Him. This refusal has eternal consequences.

Question 4: What prayer should I pray to follow a good example and avoid the bad example?

Answer: This is where the help of the Holy Spirit shines through. He surely will pray through you the things you need according to the will of God. This is a very important part of having the quiet time. This is a daily routine to help us stay in tune with the Lord. As we mature, God will lead us into deeper things for His glory. To grow in Him we must cultivate the habit of speaking with the Lord and listening to Him.

ENRICHMENT

*L*ook carefully as Yeti and I perused the scriptures that morning? His own did not receive Him. But I do receive Him. My family receives Him. Then came the crowning thought, which holds for all. "But as many as received Him, to them gave He the power to become sons of God." There is nothing more exciting, nothing more certain, nothing more satisfying than this. I have been given the power to become a child of God. This is what I started enjoying at the university. Yeti found time to do this with me for quite some time. There was nothing I longed for more than this. Gradually, my mind was getting opened to the Word.

Doing the Word, loving one another was no longer a burden. Before now, there was a kind deed girls in the fellowship were doing for many of us. They would bring in clothes from the line if it rained in our absence. Now I understand. It was a normal thing for a caring heart to do. I had been given a new heart at conversion. This is the greatest power in the universe—the power to change sinful lives.

There were many of us. We had a sweet fellowship with each other. We had days of corporate worship in our worship center, the Agric Foyer. Students from various departments, whose lives had been changed, met on various evenings for singing, prayers, and Bible study. We invited many friends to these meetings, and God kept saving souls. These were anointed meetings. Some of the other students didn't understand our new lives, and they spread various stories about us. Some said we'd lost our minds. Some said we had acquired a new kind of religion. They christened us "the new lifers." It was okay to be called that, because we had received a new life. Hallelujah!

There was a British missionary named Reverend S. G. Elton. He was one of the most frequent preachers to the fellowship on Sundays. I can still see him telling us to contend earnestly for God's Word and pull the power of the world to come into today. We sought after God; we didn't just attended services. The choir sang, and we had the Spirit come down often when we sang. We had the precious quartet. The Spirit of the Lord was among us. It was a common sight to see brethren going about campus with study Bibles among their textbooks. Those were days of Heaven on Earth.

The bleachers of our sports arena were the site of some of the many prayers brethren prayed at night after classes. The power of God was present on that campus, although it was not a Bible college. It became more than a Bible college. We prayed for wisdom. We dissected the scriptures and followed their precepts. Notable among our favorite books was the book of Ephesians.

"That the God of our Lord Jesus Christ, the Father of glory, may give unto you the spirit of wisdom and revelation in the knowledge of him: The eyes of your understanding being enlightened; that ye may know what is the hope of his calling, and what the riches of the glory of his inheritance in the saints, And what is the exceeding greatness of his power to us-ward who believe, according to the working of his mighty power, Which he wrought in Christ when he raised him from the dead and set him at his own right hand in the heavenly places, Far above all principality, and power, and might, and dominion, and every name that is named, not only in this world but also in that which is to come: And hath put all things under his feet, and gave him to be the head over all things to the church, Which is his body, the fullness of him that filleth all in all" (Eph.1:17–23).

Paul talked about our being seated in heavenly places with Christ Jesus, far above principalities and powers. For lack of personal study of God's word, some believers think they are not seated there. That is where we're still seated, waiting for the rapture of the church. While waiting for Him, we are listening to Him, fulfilling our calling in Christ Jesus our Lord.

We had various sub-groups, like village evangelism teams and Bible study prep groups. I see some of those fervent ones in village evangelism on Facebook. Some went on to study theology and have been greatly involved in world missions. Peter and his wife spent years in Capro. Many others are serving the Lord all over the world. We prayed in groups, served, and loved from the heart. Though we had come from various denominational backgrounds, we found the unity of the spirit and loved each other with unfeigned love. Love is still a hallmark of the Christian faith.

There was a sweet refrain from week to week: "Oh, Brother Emeka was saved today. Oh, Sister Eka has been saved." Countless names are on heaven's roll because this fellowship was there. Do you remember the seventies, when there was an outpouring of the Spirit on God's work in Africa? Glorious days. We are expecting a revisit of the Spirit before the close of the age. There was no taping of prayers. We prayed unto the Lord. We did not have light effects to turn on the Spirit. "For that which is born of the flesh is flesh and that which is born of the Spirit is spirit." John 3:6

We also ate together, prayed, and played together. We celebrated our birthdays and enjoyed meals that some of the parents brought. This was some fifty years ago, and all of us can confidently say, it was a most positive influence. However, some young men tried to come in with sheep's clothing, but they were ravenous wolves. God still gave victory. The whole purpose of these young men was to take advantage of the girls. Some of us who were there at that time have started going home to Heaven. Many have experienced glorious exits.

A PERSONAL MIRACLE

*O*ur lives in the fellowship were filled with various miracles that encouraged our hearts. You have read about a few of the things I experienced firsthand.

We believed in and practiced divine healing. Among many other cases of healing, one was very outstanding. I had an occasional frontal headache that defied medication very often. This pain was so intense that I would walk on the bed and tables, seeking relief. I could hardly be rational. In this particular case, the president of the fellowship asked many of the brethren to come and pray for me. Many people did lay hands on me and pray at different times. But when a particular sister laid her hands on me and prayed, there was an immediate calm. It felt like ice water was poured over my burning head. There was immediate healing from then till now, about fifty years.

He is Jehovah Rapha. He is the God who heals. I have freedom from migraine. Others can't imagine what that feels like.

That proved to me that, according to 1 Corinthians 12, there are still individuals God has endowed with gifts of healing and different other gifts.

> "Have all the gifts of healing? do all speak with tongues? Do all interpret?" (1 Cor. 12:30).

If the church could identify people with gifts and use them in the areas of their gifting, the body would be healthier and happier. God divides the gifts severally as He wills. The disciples were just fishermen. The gifts of the Spirit are not given as degrees from colleges. These gifts are not for show. These gifts are not for sale. God gives to us to help the body. If more people exercise their spiritual gifts humbly, more people in the body of Christ will be helped. How will you find your gift? God will make it manifest as you serve the body of Christ. The Lord still honors the prayers of elders according to James 5. He has healed me in answer to those too.

PERSECUTIONS FOR THE FAITH

*S*ome of us experienced extreme persecutions for our faith, as students on a university campus. Some of us experienced threats from our parents, who thought we should denounce our close walk with the Lord. They threatened to withdraw their financial support if we didn't. But the most common one I knew was sexual harassment from some professors. A notable professor, Dr. Ade, was the son of a bishop who let hell loose. He spoke out openly in class against the Christian faith. He once met me as I was carrying books to the library in the evening and stopped to talk. His car was steaming. I was standing for hours while he kept talking. What was so important, one may ask? He was trying to persuade me to agree to an illicit affair with him. I politely declined his advances, and after great frustration, he left angrily. Some other girls suffered from his hand too. But let me quickly add that God avenged all he oppressed, many years after we left Ife. While our family was living in San Ramon, California, I heard serious news. A military regime had arisen in the country and did some purging in the nation. Dr.

Ade was the first Nigerian to be retired for sexual immorality with students. Consequently, he left the country, and he met his maker by and by.

In the department of chemistry, all the male students who would speak with us girls were his targets as enemies. At least he treated them as such. He tortured them by failing them. This was not in today's world, where you would only repeat courses. Failure meant repeating a whole year. Where was our God, a very present help in trouble? He was still there, and He delivered us in unexplainable ways. Each of us has a story. We had many prayer requests on the passing of examinations. We had been taught of the steadfastness of Daniel, who would not defile himself with the King's portion. The Holy Spirit was working mightily in us. We were not going to be defiled.

The story of my conversion was all over the campus. My daily Bible reading during my quiet times helped me. We had our meetings at least twice a week, besides unstructured visits from the brethren. God was building us up. Once, in the lab, when I was busy on my project, Dr. Ade came in. In his usual flirtatious ways, he talked and talked. He told me the brothers were not around and I could sneak out with him in his car. I told him my allegiance was not to people but God. He threw his lighted cigarette on my head and walked away. Who could one report to? We shared our ordeals with God and the brethren. Those were not days of cell phones, where events could be captured. The chemistry department was adjacent to the computer department. We could see gigantic computers in their laboratory. Who could have thought that technology would come to this? Cell phones now have the capability of computers. All of these were absent, but we had God, who kept more accurate records than any on earth.

The boys in the department had their share of the persecutions. Ike's story was also very depressing. God gave him the victory. He graduated from the university and went on to marry, raise his family, and preach the Word. Melvin had his ordeals too. It was not only in the science department, but the details would take volumes. Who would believe our report?

I had failed a year and it was a devastating blow. I was not a student of average intelligence. My mother and my five siblings were waiting far away in the East, and I could not afford to be expelled from the university. Many were told, "From your inability to benefit from university education, you have been advised to withdraw." This was the fate of all who had repeated their classes for two years. My situation caught God's attention, and He appeared on the scene. Hallelujah. Unimaginable. Inexpressible. God would do a thing like that! He did, He did. There is nothing He can't do if He wants to.

A Divine Messenger in the
Morning at Yaba Lagos

The summer of 1974 was different. We had finished the semester's exams. I felt happy that I had done my best. Some of the students stayed back on campus to work on their final projects. I went down to Lagos to visit my friend Louisa and to look for a summer job. The environment of this city was rowdy and challenging, but I was determined to join in the hustle. The next morning, I got ready to go downtown from Yaba and begin my job search. I hung my purse on my shoulder and sat down on the cushion getting ready to leave for Lagos. Suddenly I went into a trance.

I had a vision. I was told, "Go back to Ile Ife. You've been asked to withdraw, but the Lord has prevailed. When you go, you will see Dr. Olu. He will send you to Dr. Ogu, and I will give you victory."

This sounded so strange. I'd never heard or read of such an occurrence except in the Bible. Remember, I'd been a born-again Christian for only three years at this point. I believed the vision was from God. I did not tell even Louisa, in whose house I was. That was from fear of being discouraged. I went out to the street, took a taxi, and headed to the university. In a couple of hours, I was in Ile Ife.

I am humbly talking about the God who has graciously involved Himself in my little business that no one on earth could have helped with. This testimony should encourage the true lovers of God to know, believe, trust, and expect God to deliver them in dire circumstances, whereby earth cannot prevail. Many people believe there is no God and that, if He does exist, He doesn't get interested in the things that happen on earth. No, no, no. There is a God who intervenes in the causes of the oppressed. Let us please rekindle our lamps. Let us expect the God of Heaven to have His way in our lives. The truth may be called falsehood, and the fake may appear like truth, but there is a God. I know He sees all, knows all, and can decide to intervene anytime, anywhere.

My feet were strengthened. My heart was comforted. I was excitedly looking forward to what God would do. It was not difficult for me to take that trip back to the university. I couldn't wait to get to the department. Who would blame me, with the God of the Universe behind me? There is no greater wealth than having God. He comes through even when we don't know the danger we're in.

"The angel of the Lord encamps around those that fear the Lord and delivers them" (Ps. 34:7).

The Lord's Uplifted Hand

I went straight to our department and what did I see? Many of my classmates saw me on the way in and began to sympathize with me. "Oh, we're so sorry at what has befallen you," some said. "Don't accept it," some said.

Within a short period, a crowd of students had surrounded me. But in my heart, I found joy because the Lord had gone ahead of me. As I reached the entrance into the department, who did I see? It was Dr. Olu, standing with outstretched hands on the lintel.

He addressed me as I was about to enter the department. "Oh, we're so sorry for what has happened to you." I jumped in on that. Then, on his own he said, "Okay, you better see Dr. Ogu. Are you seeing the trail? Is there a God who is all-seeing, all-knowing, and almighty?"

But it happened to me. Through quite a trail, I was sent to the office of the departmental head, Professor Ed, an American from the state of Utah. I was shocked. As soon as I walked into his room he said, "Sit down, Vic. Stop crying. It's the fault of some of your

Nigerian lecturers, who don't know how to differentiate between their love life and their work." He called me by name. That surprised me. I never knew that he knew my name.

That was not a culture where students are very free with their professors. I didn't take any of his classes. He must have heard my story beforehand, because I never told him my story. He went on to tell me how watching my life in the department had impressed him. Seated with him was one of the students from Sierra Leone. He said I should come with her to his home in the evening for some corn. In my heart I thought, "Is this time for corn?" I thanked him but declined the offer. He was sincere, but I was burdened and wanted to spend that time with the Lord. He promised to take care of my result. He went out and called on Dr. Rhi and another professor, whose name I have forgotten. Together they held the master sheet on the corridor and changed my result. Surely it came to pass. That was the exalted hand of the Lord.

He is a revealer of secrets, and there is nothing He cannot do. "The secret things belong unto the Lord our God: but those things which are revealed belong unto us and to our children forever" (Deut. 29:29).

No man can successfully fight against God. There is no record of such a thing. Some apparent failures are opportunities for God to show His glory.

Without the revelation, I could not have known that I'd been failed. Wow! I could have been busy in Lagos only to find out later that I'd been dismissed from the university. What tongue can a mortal use in this age to tell me there is no God? No never!

I went into my final year and did my best to graduate. How can I not tell this story? Whatever mortals would say about this does not matter. I owe my allegiance to the Lord, who takes permission from no man to bless a person. It happened to me, so I know. I try to reflect on the difference this divine intervention made in my family and in my life. I shudder to imagine that the contrary could have been possible. Where would I be today?

I owe God this tribute. It is worth my shout out to this world. I think back and shudder at such mercies. Please join me to sing a song to the Lord as you read this account. God made me leave the university in triumph. I am a witness that there is a living God who is active in the lives of humanity. There is the supernatural. You can renew your faith in Him, or you can establish your faith in Him. These revelations are certainly meant to help shine a light more and more on our paths.

The point to note is that this is God taking the initiative to reveal a thing. There are people of some persuasions who go about looking for people to tell them secret things. That has gotten a lot of people caught in the snares of false prophets. Hebrews 1:2–3 says God has spoken unto us by His Son. If He chooses to use any additional means, it's up to Him. Faith works. It is not fiction. This is the same Almighty Spirit that revealed this to the apostle Paul.

"How that by revelation he made known unto me the
mystery; (as I wrote afore in few words, Whereby,
when ye read, ye may understand my knowledge
in the mystery of Christ) Which in other ages was

not made known unto the sons of men, as it is now revealed unto his holy apostles and prophets by the Spirit; That the Gentiles should be fellow heirs, and of the same body, and partakers of his promise in Christ by the gospel" (Eph. 3:3–6).

The purpose is always that those who have not known the way may know and learn to follow Jesus the Lord. It's a gift of grace. So many things of supernatural dimensions have happened in this world to further the cause of righteousness, and we can only capture a few on the pages of books. Some false things have been attributed to Him, the Lord. But as a guide, everything God does supernaturally aligns with Scripture. Do not believe anything deviant, no matter how many people say it.

The new session at the university was a very encouraging one. Think of the impact that divine intervention made in my life and those of fellow believers. And many more joined in the discipleship project. Many brothers and sisters whose names are known to the Lord, did follow-up, too, on the new converts. Brethren just took younger believers under their wings. It was a common sight to see students sit in twos, threes, or more on stairs to lecture rooms or halls discussing the Word. There was no compulsion. It was only joy unspeakable and full of glory.

These mini discussions were personal. We formed groups of friends with each other. I remember how Sisters Comfort and Moji looked out for me after Sister Yetunde graduated and left the university. Other sisters helped me too. Everybody who knew us thought Brother Ekpe was my boyfriend, but that was farthest from the truth. He was one of those who encouraged me, prayed for me, and answered my questions. We came from the same ethnic group as a few others. It was pure joy when you learned that someone so close to home got saved.

Some relationships just happened. Iyabo and Oluremi (recently a presidential candidate in Nigeria) were my younger friends and sisters. God helped me watch out for them. We prayed together often, read the Word, and sang praises. It would take more books to narrate what God did for us. There was the biological garden where we found solace. Sometimes a roommate could not stand the constant stream of brethren coming to visit. We had to exercise restraint and take some fellowship time outdoors. Some of those relationships still endure. Many of the relationships became lifelong. A lot of young men found their spouses in the group.

The institute of marriage is for the good of man. Children enjoy a sense of security in a solid home.

Therefore shall a man leave his father and his mother, and shall cleave to his wife: and they shall be one flesh.

Two people who have a common faith in the Word of God can very often live peacefully in marriage if they adhere to God's Word. I have proved this and observed it in many believers.

Some of those campus relationships matured into marriages. Healthy homes resulted, where a new dynamic generation is being raised. For the living, it's good to keep praying for one another. It's the will of God. Wherever you started the journey, there must have been others alongside you. Do you remember them? It's most important on your knees. These relationships have endured.

The Gospel of Jesus is redemptive. Some friends who were careless over God's words have found mercy through repentance. God has put their lives back on the right track. You can find God's mercy with the husband of your youth or the wife of your youth.

Sandra's Two Weeks

I must squeeze in this story before I conclude this bit. Before my conversion in 1971, I had some white and black American friends with whom I was proud to identify. They had come to the university in exchange programs from the US. One of them was Sandra, who taught me how to be careful with stuff. She had lent me a needle and I misplaced it. She bothered me so much until I bought a new one for her. She told me how she worked for everything she had and was planning to be a career girl. I didn't understand then, but I'm now in America.

The fun part was how she taught me to hitchhike. At first, it was a scary thought. Supposing the driver took me to some other place. But society was more predictable then. I would stand with her by the roadside, and we'd just get rides to wherever. That was new to me. One of the weekends, we hitchhiked to a Shrine where Iya Osun was, in Osogbo. We toured the shrine and she showed such interest, talking with the Iya (mother of the shrine). I could never have undertaken such a trip on my own. We of African origin take such issues very seriously. Students from my home state never knew where I was all that day. I come from a close-knit community, and someone would have looked for me in my absence.

I'd developed a relationship with Sandra. There were issues the young American students discussed among themselves. One would talk about shooting up drugs and getting high. Thank God they never asked me to join them. In my naivety, I could have been hooked to drugs, and who knows, my path may have taken a detour. Our great God shielded me, even in the days of my ignorance. God loves the children of men

You can imagine Sandra's disappointment when she heard I was at a revival meeting all day Saturday 16, 1971. She came down to my room and made a bet with me. She said, "Vi, I bet you'll get over this in two weeks. You're not the religious type."

By the grace of God, Sandra's two weeks have not yet expired, from January 1971 till 2020. It will expire when the Lord calls me home. What a dependable Savior! Please let us join hands to tell the world of a Savior who came from glory, died for all, and loves all men. He wants all men to repent and trust in Him as their Savior. I long to know what happened to Sandra.

God can keep. He has kept me in my marriage for forty-six years and still counting.

In Ile Ife, after each generation of ECU leaves, the work keeps increasing in leaps and bounds. May we all pray, "Thy Kingdom come, thy will be done on earth as it is in heaven." There is a place of prayer, prevailing prayers, in the conversion of souls like mine. This was a time when the Holy Spirit was moving over the different university campuses in Africa. The other universities, like the University of Ibadan, Ahmadu Bello University in Zaria, University of Nigeria Nsukka, had campus fellowships where God was working too, by His Spirit. During the long vacations, we teamed up and gave a battle shout for the King. The Spirit moves everywhere when men pray. He is not confined to campuses. Some of the products of these campus fellowships have gone on to do mighty deeds for the Lord. Big churches with sound doctrine built around Holy living have been established across the continents. Many experienced men of God sowed into our lives. Those were days when we prayed well before singing our solos, duets, quartets, etc. People wept under the conviction of the Spirit. It was not showmanship. Awake, people of God, the impending doom I was warned to flee from may be right around the corner. Weep for lost souls. Let us examine ourselves to see if we are in the faith.

Our Lord is coming again. "Watch ye therefore: for ye know not when the master of the house cometh, at even, or at midnight, or at the cockcrowing, or in the morning" (Matt. 13:35).

Just as we received the Gospel, we must take hold of God's grace to remain vigilant. Since prophecies concerning His birth, crucifixion, and resurrection have been fulfilled, the return of Jesus will be fulfilled. That many of us are married and settled does not mean we should throw vigilance out the window. He will return. We will see Him. He said Occupy till I come.

LIVING SINGLE AND BUSY

When the long vacation came, and we went back home after my salvation, the fire in my soul did not let me sit still. I teamed up with others, like Comfort and Udofot, to go about witnessing to high schools. Many of the products of those days are still serving the Lord. Christian students from many universities gathered in their regions to tell the good news of Jesus. Those were wonderful days of singlehood. I enjoyed those. I also enjoy these days of married life. But I can't compare marriage to the liberty of going and going and going for the Lord. Wherever He has kept us, His grace is sufficient. May we not complicate the Gospel of Jesus.

The First Major Challenge

Those were days of fire in our hearts. I miss the fire and pray for its return. Do you remember? I began to look differently on all the writings on buses and businesses. There were captions on businesses like, "No man like God." Or: "Gifts come from God."

I wondered if the people who wrote these understood the depth of their words. This was after coming home on holidays. I would muse about these things in my heart. Then I first went to my church bishop and asked him questions. "Why did Martin Luther, who brought the Reformation, teach us that the just shall live by faith as it says in Romans 1:17. Why did no one teach us that?"

We had daily chapel meetings in our mission high school. The reverend told me not to get into such details. How could my heart be quieted by any man when I was on a race, fleeing from impending doom? He told me that a group of nurses from the nursing school in Anua, five miles away, had done shamefully. He said they would stand in the city square and talk about all their old lives. Little did he know that he was introducing me to new friends, I sought them out and found out that the Spirit had opened their blind eyes to the Gospel. Our circle of friends now expanded. We continued in aggressive witnessing for Jesus. That was our source of joy. The fruits still abound.

I had overworked and was exhausted one weekend. Sometimes fervent praying takes strength. I could only whisper. The young people who were getting born again posed a threat to the kingdom of darkness. We too were witnesses, like the disciples of old. We had the home of Uncle Edet G. Utuk and his wife, Monica, as a base. This couple had been Christians around our area before we came back from the university with our excitement concerning the new life. Uncle Utuk attended Nigeria's premier school, the University of Ibadan. He had been part of the university fellowship in Ibadan. He let his light shine, and we heard of his testimony and that of his wife, Monica. Women were talking of the kind lady nurse at the mission hospital in Etinan. A light that is set upon a hill cannot be hidden.

An Angel from Heaven

*T*his was my first long vacation after my salvation. I was a guest of the Utuk family. He was then a vice principal at Etinan Institute, a high school that has produced governors and gifted preachers. He and his lovely wife, Monica, maintained an open home for many. They served as mentors for a lot of us young Christians from the Southeast.

I'd spent over a week in their home. My days were filled with witnessing, in the company of other young people, for Jesus. I was very sick one night, and the couple came and prayed over me, committing me to God's healing and keeping power. I remember their soft, faith-filled, simple prayers.

> "Fear thou not for I am with thee, be not dismayed; for I am thy God: I will strengthen thee: yea, I will help thee; yea, I will uphold thee with the right hand of my righteousness" (Isa. 41:10).

After I'd slept for a time, I was awakened by a bright light in the room. An angel that looked like gold stood across the room with lifted hands. He said, "Cheers. I have been sent to tell you the Lord is with you. When you awake, read Joshua 1:9."

I woke up completely well. Remember, I was a young Christian. I could not easily find the book of Joshua. The Bible is a living book. I was overjoyed when I finally found the passage.

> "Have not I commanded thee? Be strong and of a good courage; be not afraid, neither be thou dismayed: for the LORD thy God is with thee whithersoever thou goest" (Josh. 1:9).

Who would not trust and serve a God like this? The encouragement I received was over the roof. No one can imagine what this divine encounter did for my soul and still does. As you can see, I never went seeking all the visitations of Heaven, but God just chose to deal thus with me. This is pure grace. He does not have to deal with some other in this way, but He gets to all His children. I'm so thankful that I have Jesus in my heart. Are you not happy to have a God so great?

God truly helps us along the journey. Even when we reach terrible roadblocks, He is still God, the I Am.

A Witness to My Family

The story of my salvation resonated a lot with my family. I first invited my brother closest to me in age to come with me to a crusade at Irete, in the Aba Owerri area of Nigeria. He had started petty trading after high school and was happy to think of things to buy that he could sell in Aba. None of that happened. I took him to a camp in Irete. He was very challenged by the glorious testimonies of handsome undergraduates from various places. He prayed and was beautifully saved before our return home. He is still in the faith today, despite all of life's challenges. The difference in his life was clear.

One of my aunties said to me, "What new religion have you brought from Aba?"

All my other siblings came to a saving knowledge of Jesus by and by. A little light brightens the darkness. The effect of this is a transgenerational effect of raising families in the fear and admonition of the Lord.

He saves one and saves the rest of the family. Even those who backslide will come back.

My mother was a church mother in our previous church denomination. She was a counselor to many women in helping to raise children. No one could argue, since she had raised the six of us as a widow. It took a few years for my mother to finally see the difference between nominal Christianity and a faith founded on repentance. But it finally happened. She had many useful years of serving the Lord after her new birth. We have a legacy of a praying mom. Some of the answers to her prayers are yet to manifest. When she was laid to rest, we knew she went home to her Lord Jesus.

Through God's providential care He made a way for my brother Uko to travel to the US for studies. God established him. The rest of my siblings all love the Lord. I had not married then. The family continued working hard with my mother as the breadwinner.

THE GOD WHO MOVES AT
APPOINTED TIMES

*T*he Lord gave me a husband by the time I graduated from college. I went to the science department, and fortunately, I met Dr. Ade. I introduced him to my husband. It was a battle won for the King of Kings. My husband drove me in our new Toyota Corolla from the University of Ife to our town, Uyo, to meet my mother. My traditional marriage had been conducted in my absence while I was still in school. It was so done because I needed a court certificate to show the National Youth Service Corps secretariat to rescind my posting from Lagos to Uyo. It is a requirement that every college graduate under age forty must first serve the country for one year in some other state. We were very madly in love and could have been plying the unsafe, windy road between Lagos and Uyo (427 miles) more than once a month. Who knows what could have happened?

Thank God we obtained the transfer. We were able to wed later in July of the same year. Our wedding was a great one. Our parents were there, except Dad, who had passed when I was still a teenager. Our brethren came in a coaster bus from the West—more than thirty of them. A few came on their own. Emeka and Bade drove in their new car, bringing Iyabo Williams (Ogunaike) along. Remember, I'd graduated only in June, and the brethren just came to my wedding with excitement. We had brought Stella Ekpe (Akenova). The brethren in Uyo saw love in action. The brethren helped out—cooking, decorating, running errands, going between Ndiya (my birthplace) and Uyo. We went to Aba for last-minute shopping and much more. My late sister-in-law, Mrs. Atim Ekanem, was so busy with catering that she was absent from all the wedding pictures. I'm talking about a wedding over forty-five years ago. I answered a lot of questions from the church because they needed to be sure that my husband, their beloved brother, was marrying a Christian woman. We laugh at some of those ordeals now. But few people knew that we had individually sought God's face in prayers for up to two years before committing to each other. Let me share a funny story.

Miss Jonah

*E*tekamba means "the big man." It's a name of endearment. I have called him that since our wedding. He'd sent a message that he would come to the University of Ife from Ibadan, his university, to visit. I planned to run and hide so he wouldn't find me. This was before I surrendered and said yes to him. I left my room and went to Jumoke's room, in the postgraduate block, to hide. I covered my face and lay there resting on a Saturday. Little did I know that Richard, the fiancé of Jumoke, in whose room I hid, had sent a message to Jumoke. Out of the blue, somebody entered the room and started calling out Jumoke's name. I heard his voice and felt like disappearing. After hearing no response, he uncovered my face gently, thinking it was Jumoke, but it was Victoria, the Jonah. He said gently, "Victoria, how have you treated me this way?" and my heart melted. I loved him and I was sorry to have behaved childishly. I apologized. He accepted it.

Thank God I stuck with him. Here I am today, forty-six years later, happy and content in the Lord. So you can know how gentle he became after he started going to scripture union camps, I must tell this story.

When I went to meet his people before our wedding, his eldest sister said something to me. "Victoria, what did my brother say to you? How did he approach you?" This was because she didn't believe her brother could talk about love for a girl. He appeared too holy to talk of love. But love at the right time is part of the package. But he did to me, blessed Vic.

GOD'S PROVISION

How did we get money for the wedding? Our friends came to the rescue. We never solicited any help, but friends just took the initiative.

Love each other like brethren, the Word admonishes. This was what we received.

> "Distributing to the necessity of the saints; given to hospitality" (Rom. 12:13).

God again showed up. One brother offered to pay for our wedding cake. Another volunteered to pay for the drinks. The sewing of my wedding dress was a gift. Many teamed up to cook the food for the wedding. I pray that acts of kindness will never depart from the body of Christ.

Let's go back to the wedding day. The church sent musicians in the church bus—violinists, trumpeters, you name it. They played beautiful tunes on the way from Ikot Ekpene to Uyo, about twenty miles apart. Etekamba and I were highly favored. The wedding was conducted by the district overseer, Reverend S. E. Ekanem.

The reception was a highlight, and we sang a duet with my husband, "Great Is Thy Faithfulness." Indeed, great is God's faithfulness. The missionary outfit in Ikwa, Ikot Abasi, had prepared to host us for our honeymoon. It was kept a secret until after the wedding vows. Lo and behold, we went off after the wedding without taking care of our guests, who had come with us from across our land. I was excited to go and rest at Ikwa, but when I got there, I had other sets of problems. How do I come out of the room for breakfast? What are the people at the table, holy missionaries, thinking of me? See how childish I still was? There was nothing new at the age of twenty-four. Thank God for God. My quiet husband was there, not saying much, not asking what was going on in my mind, but I went through it and survived.

It was not "they lived happily ever after" but the normal ups and downs of every young Christian couple. One thing was at the front of my days, God had a purpose in our lives. There were too many pointers. A particular one was the prayers over us the day before we left the university. There was an elderly man of God who had come in from England and was praying with the Christian fellowship. We just came in from Uyo to join. He had spoken a word of knowledge over us. Awesome things! After forty-five years, I still remember. Thank God for His Holy Spirit. His miraculous interventions in my life, in salvation and graduation, nudged me always to be available for God. Marriage was not settling down. It was more like being pilgrims on a journey. Thus far, what stood out strong for me? Nothing can replace the personal intentional time alone with God. A lot of guidance came on the back of those prayer times and still does.

Challenges and God's Sufficiency

*M*y husband continued full-time with schooling after we were married, working here and there. The babies had started coming, and I kept at home with them, working as a teacher. I mean I didn't go ahead to further my postgraduate work, but I allowed my husband to go on. My third posting after finishing the National Youth Service Corps (NYSC) was as a young principal in a girls high school in Ikot Ebak. It was almost a pioneering work. The tests were many. I had to seek God's face in prayer, and I taught many of those teen girls to pray. And because the Lord opened the door, many of those young people were saved.

This school was built very far away from human activity. I'd worked there for more than a year before the commissioner for education approved a generator to be given to us. You can only imagine the pitch darkness starting at seven each night. The cooing of birds and chattering of crickets were constants. In the rainy seasons, we had the croaking of toads and frogs. Those sounds from nature kept us company. We had night watchmen, using lanterns at night to find their way. There was a clear stream running beside the school compound. It was a great resort kind of place. Huge, dangerous snakes lived by the waters. There was hardly a week when we did not see snake marks and scales left on the dirt paths. Remember, this was a girls' high school. It was also a boarding school. The real testimony is that no student or staff was ever bitten by a snake. Many of those tropical snakes are very poisonous. We heard different birds cooing at sundown. I still held on to the promise of Joshua: "Be strong and of good courage" (Josh. 1:9). I needed every bit of courage to survive in this terrain with my young children. Remember, girl students were living on campus too. What protection can a wooden fence provide? That was all we had.

The only place I could visit for a change of scene was the local church, some six miles away. I had dynamic pastors who didn't have a lot of this world's education but had a grasp of God's Word. There are sermons I still remember. As lively stones, we're built into a great edifice for God. One can't be a lump of clay and pretend to be a stone. Stones are stacked on stones, with Jesus Christ being the chief cornerstone—the foundation. Does that idea not send some joy welling up your veins? We had the privilege of going for camp meetings with the girls. God worked, and the fruits still endure.

THE NIGHTMARE AND GOD'S VOICE

There was a night when one of my young sons had a nightmare and spoke in his sleep. "Mom please take the hoe from them. They want to bury me."

Who wanted to bury my young son? What did he know about burying? He was no more than four years old. Unbelievable. What would any mother do? I got up and reassured him that nobody could bury him. He slept again.

I entered into God's throne room of mercy in intercession. I prayed and wept out my heart before the Lord. My house team also prayed, all young girls. After I'd prayed for a considerable amount of time, something out of this world happened. Suddenly a huge Bible with gold trim descended into the room. I still have the shivers as I write about it. It was opened to Isaiah, chapter 44, with the scarlet ribbon hanging down. I was raised to the level of the big book. An unspoken communication ensued. There was a being whose face I could not see. I only saw the back and shoulder and the hand that was pointing to the Scriptures. The figure started reading. "Who confirms the word of His servant, And performs the counsel of His messengers" (Isa. 44:26).

I read along with this heavenly being, who said, "You must not sit here and cry. You have to speak what you want. It is God's place to confirm your word. People cry as they pray in repentance. When you meet challenges, you use your words to say what you want to be done. God will then confirm your word. Look at the scripture, and see what Elijah did to glorify the Lord when he was confronted by a problem."

This being from Heaven, which I can call an angel, continued the lecture. I can only paraphrase it now, since it was some time ago. I feel unburdened, because I now know that I have shared this important message. This lecture took more than an hour. The message continued as the angel told me about what happened in Los Angeles, when the Holy Spirit was poured forth on a praying remnant. I kept peeping into the big Bible. There were many questions in my heart. Whatever question I raised was answered immediately. All of this was an unspoken communication.

I raised the point that I was a woman, and no one would listen to me. That was when the angel told me about the outpouring in Los Angeles. He said women were involved, and they carried the message. I told the angel that the denomination I worshipped with would never allow me to share this. I said, "You're going to make me a false prophet." I never dreamed that I would ever have an opportunity to share this with the reading world. I feel relieved that I've shared this piece. But I've shared this message at a local level many times. Over these many years, I have felt indebted to the church.

It is important to know that we have a God who confirms the words of His servants. I know the burden that has been on the shoulders of God's people, as an unbelieving world surrounds them to see if the Jesus they preach about can perform the works of old. It's not a show, but there are times of dire need, and God will come through. My experience has been this. When we call upon Him with a single heart, without anything else at the back of our minds, God comes through. Many saints in Christendom can use this verse. That night, that angel told me to "tell the Church." Oh, how happy I am to be alive to tell. God confirms the word of His servants.

The God I know shows up in miraculous ways when He sees a need.

The vision I had that night has proved useful in critical situations. I've measured my expectations against this verse many times. There have been situations in my life in which I haven't always obeyed that verse. But I continue to seek the Lord, and He leads me on. That word I was given worked for my young son under those particular circumstances. As our abiding becomes more perfect, God will grant the desires of our hearts according to His will.

God will not let anyone boast in His presence. The young teenage girls who prayed with me are now grandmothers, and the torch of faith still shines. This is the takeaway from that dangerous terrain, that school. I learned courage. The natives showed their fight against my faith. God defended His name. A certain incident stands out as an example of how they showed their opposition. It was during a season when different communities organized vigilante groups to protect their villages from robbers. It was late at night, and I was returning from my mother's station, where she was teaching. When I arrived at this particular checkpoint, a few miles from our school, the vigilante group would not let me pass. They blocked our school bus, which was carrying me to go back from my mother's school. The night watchmen said they would not allow me to pass because I never allow men to come into the school compound and talk to my students, the girls. Horrible! My labor pains had started. It took about an hour at that place in the deep darkness. But God helped us, using a few dissenting voices in the darkness. "Allow her pass, she is in labor."

A Night Vision

That baby was born by the miraculous intervention of the Highest. The pains I'd felt at the checkpoint were false labor pains. It took up to one more week before the real labor pains came on. My husband was away at the university working on his postgraduate work. Let me share another true story here. I didn't tell you that my coming back to my isolated school compound was in response to my pastor's call. Before, I'd always had very difficult labor. My pastor had taken up my delivery as a challenge. This was the first time I was going to give birth in this station. He had prayed with selected elders until God gave him assurance of victory for me. One night, toward the expected date of delivery, I had a vision. A majestic being in a doctor's coat came into my room. She greeted me and said, "I've been sent to work on you so you have no excessive pain at childbirth."

I could see the being and my room. I laid down, and she removed a curved object around her neck and started scrapping between my legs. I was watching it. When she finished, she said, "Let us thank the Lord." We knelt together and she raised her hands as we praised God for His love.

I said, "Could you pray over me?"

The being said, "I was only sent to work on you. I was not sent to pray over you." I count it a great privilege to have had this encounter with Heaven.

The angel said, "Let me tell you about the nature of messages in Heaven. We do the Father's bidding. We do not do anything that He does not order. " This has encouraged me to listen to divine counsel and prayerfully follow through. What does the Good Book, the Bible say?

> "Thy will be done as in heaven, so on earth"
> (Luke 11:2b).

Learn to follow divine counsel.

God Still Guides

*T*his concept also showed up in my husband's choice for his postgraduate work. He sent word that he was changing his master's work from analytical chemistry, where he had already spent one year, to petroleum geochemistry. I was initially upset, because it meant a longer time waiting with the children for his return. He had sought the face of the Lord with his friends, Mabel, Ibukun, Kayode, and more. But as a result of his changing to petroleum geochemistry, he was working under his classmate. It did not bother him. He was intent on work, as led by the Lord. As a result of this change, he was sent to Julich, Germany, to finish his doctorate. We had gotten our first three children at this time. I was able to visit him in Germany and travel to the US for the first time. Most significant is the relocation of our family to the US.

"The steps of a righteous man are ordered by the Lord and He delighted in his way" (Ps. 37:23).

After his graduation, he returned to our home state, in Southeast Nigeria, to teach at the University of Calabar. Our family was united under a roof again and was serving the Lord with the church. We both spent our weekends translating the Sunday school materials into our language. The weekend was when many people found time to do second jobs. I asked my husband many times, "Won't you look for a second job?" My husband always said, "The Lord will provide for us." Despite his qualification and the fact that we were a two-income family, life was not smooth. Those looking at us from the outside could never tell. My husband was fond of bringing guests with him when coming back from work. I, therefore, had to make a little extra food, to accommodate whoever would come.

On this bright day, all I had was five naira, which is less than a dime now, but it was up to five dollars then. I sent for iced fish and fresh vegetables. That was enough for a nice soup, just enough for him and the guest he may bring. I was right. He came back with a guest. I was glad that when he asked if we had food for guests, my answer was yes. The rest of the family ate some old food, and it was okay.

After his eight years of lecturing at the University of Calabar, God showed up again. We thought we were settled in life. We had siblings in the US, but we were not dreaming of leaving to join them.

But before telling about how God took us out of the university, I have to share a few highlights of His care.

Expect Prevailers at 5:00 p.m.

*I*t was in 1986, after my husband came back to Nigeria from New York, where he'd delivered a paper at an international conference of petroleum geochemists. It was a conference in April, and he thought his clothes would be okay. But he found out quickly that he was wrong. He was quaking from the cold. When he returned to Nigeria, he developed some health issues. Our doctor friend visited him at home, and I caught him weeping for my husband. I ignored it and still looked unto the Lord. For three days, he was not able to leave the bed. He could not eat, and we were very concerned.

Early the next day, when I went to check on him, he started saying unusual things. He told me to take care of the children—that he was going the way of all men. I interrupted him. I told him I didn't come to marry a man who would die and leave me with a young family. I reminded him that my father had died and left me as a teenager. Nevermore would I accept it. I left him and sent for my praying friends. They joined me in fervent intercession for him.

We had prayed for about three hours, and then God answered in a way I knew.

He sent a messenger to write just one line on a pad: "Expect prevailers at 5:00 p.m." I jumped up with joy, feeling I was back to my usual self. I didn't understand who the prevailers were. Were they going to come as angels in the realm of the spirit? Were they going to be visible or invisible? But I told my friends that God had spoken. They rejoiced with me and left.

I continued doing the normal Saturday chores. Joy filled my heart. At exactly 5:00 p.m., the big apostolic faith bus for Africa for Christ arrived at our gate. They moved like soldiers up the stairs to our flat on the third floor. They started praying. I hadn't sent for them. These were not the days of cell phones. I could never have thought of calling them. This was a Sunday evening, and they never left the headquarters to come to Calabar. So Heaven saw them as prevailers.

God knows those who prevailers are, so don't stumble over titles.

We saw them as Sunday school teachers. My husband was well immediately. He came down from the bed. He ate. There was joy in the house. We were encouraged. Many of those who prayed at that time have gone on to their eternal reward.

You may give yourself a title upon the earth. But how does Heaven know you? I felt these kinds of stories should not be lost. They should be told. We continued to live our normal lives. We spent a lot of our weekends going from Calabar to Ikot Enwang to work on translations of Sunday school materials into our local language.

An Unusual Day

*I*t was an ordinary Saturday at the beginning. Then a Peugeot station wagon pulled up the driveway. It was from Gulf Oil Company (now Chevron Oil Company). They had a letter of inquiry from the company with an offer of work. The letter was addressed to Dr. O. T. Udo, my husband. He sent for his friend, late Professor U. J. Ekpe, whose family also lived on the University of Calabar campus. We stood in the corridor and lifted the letter to the Lord in prayers. Later, he discussed it with our pastor.

My husband had not applied for this job. He was recommended for it by some professors in Germany who supervised his work in petroleum geochemistry.

He had earlier sent a paper to be read at a conference in Italy, because he had no sponsor to pay for him to attend. In the end, Chevron started looking for my husband. After the search went to Ibadan University, they were directed to him in Calabar. Remember, my husband is an Ibibio man, a minority tribe, according to the world. But the Lord had started preparing him for this job so he would fulfill God's purpose.

My husband was finally hired to start the research laboratory in Lekki, Nigeria. That work required him to go abroad to the US with his wife and five children to do more work. But before we left, we had a visit from hell.

Paid Assassins

That weekend, when my husband flew to Lagos to discuss with the management of the company, things took a turn. I traveled in the company of our two helpers, Eno and Lucy, in our station wagon to our farm on the outskirts of Calabar, more than twenty miles away. Many families owned cassava farms, to supplement the food supply for their families. We left very early, before the babies woke up. We had driven the dirt road, and we parked beside the farm. As we started reaping the cassava, we heard things falling like pebbles. Little did I know that we were then the target of a killer squad. Some soldiers had been paid to kill a certain rich woman who drove our kind of car.

We started harvesting the cassava but kept hearing things falling like pebbles. There was also a sporadic hum of a horn. When the sound got so near us, I went to the dirt road to look. There were three men there with guns pointed at me.

I innocently said, "Are you looking for an animal?" I had overheard one of them say we've found the deer.

Immediately they started giving me orders. "Don't move from there." But a scripture came to me, and God delivered me from paid assassins.

> "For by thee I have run through a troop, and by my
> God, I have leaped over a wall" (Ps. 18:29).

I remembered this particular scripture, which we'd recently studied, and it energized me.

I got the girls into the car and drove off. They fired at the car, but I just suffered minor bruises on my lips, which I knocked on the steering wheel while trying to duck.

A lot of villagers came out because they heard the gunshots. They told the whole story of how the killer squad had been lurking in the bushes waiting for that woman's car. It was a big scene in Akpabuyo. I had to wait in one of the huts till my strength returned. The squad was still pursuing us, so many men in the village went in search of them. Later that day, a woman drove by in the same light green Peugeot station wagon and stopped where I was. The villagers had told her what had happened. She hugged me and said, "You could have died in my place."

Without going into every detail of how it all went, I can say God overcame it for me. A very top family later sent an apology to us through our pastor. The villagers were pressing on us to take the case to court. The Scriptures do infuse with strength. That's why I was able to defy the threat of guns. We read in the Scriptures that women received their dead back to life again by faith. The same Jesus still does the unthinkable in the face of danger to defend His people.

That evening, my husband flew in from Lagos, where he'd gone to meet the officials of Gulf Oil Company. The work was secured, and we only waited for the official letter stating the conditions and benefits. The letter finally came. He had to resign from lecturing at the university. I no longer needed to hassle with cultivating crops to make ends meet. God delivered us from so much, but we didn't know that our children would miss their friends badly.

God Changed Our Situation for the Better

*T*here were a few options given to my husband in the offer. He could bring his wife and children at once. Another option was that he could bring the family to visit four times a year. and there were others. He picked the option to move the family to the US. That's why we're here today.

This was a privilege that many people sold their lands to obtain. But it was given to us on a silver platter. We had completely entrusted Him with our lives, and He is the I Am. My husband reported first to Lekki, in Lagos. He worked there for some time and then, in 1989, he was moved overseas to beautiful San Ramon, in northern California, and we, the children and I, joined him in 1990. I still remember the flight to New York. Gulf Oil Company had paid for six seats but when we boarded the plane, we saw that there were only five. The pilot said I could stay back and travel some other time. I could not accept that, because we had missed flying two previous times because of overbooking. I had to keep my baby on my lap. The baby was three. But I was happy we made it. My sister Ekpedeme met us with hot dogs during our brief stopover in New York. Her husband, Ene, gave us some comforting words at the welcome. But the word *dog* put us off. We had never heard of dogs for meat. I laugh looking back. We now eat hot dogs joyfully.

The next leg of the journey was to San Francisco, where Dad was waiting for us with a limousine and driver. Talk about sudden elevation in this world! This was it. Oh, we were happy. Awaiting us were plush carpeted rooms. My kitchen was standard, and I asked how to use some of the gadgets.

We were given a Crown Victoria for use while in San Ramon. There was a good community of African technocrats who worked for Chevron, and we had a great time together. But the greater fellowship was with the church brethren in San Francisco, with whom we worshipped every weekend. There was a weekly Bible study group with our colleagues in our home. That was our outreach effort to the affluent group with big oil money. Our souls come first, and we need to share the love of Jesus. Nigerians are very religious people, because a lot of our grandmas attended women fellowship in their various churches. There are a lot of born-again Christians in Nigeria, truly. Some churches still preach the unadulterated Gospel of Jesus. The Gospel asserts that without holiness, no man will see the Lord. But there is a huge problem with syncretism. Let it be clear that those who are born again love the Lord fervently. The differentiating factor is that they have a point where they were converted. They are given new hearts. They desire holiness. They are serving the Lord worldwide. But we all need to remember how the Lord has led us to places we never dreamed of. We owe Him our witness. Others have to come in. The doors of mercy are still open. Remember to invite your neighbors to the marriage supper of the Lamb!

Our Children Had a Right to Live

There was a problem with our children and their ability to adjust to a new culture, which we were not expecting. We underestimated their challenges. The children were between three and thirteen. Our only daughter was lonely. We had uprooted them from their native soil when they were just beginning to grow roots. The issue of friends is huge in the developmental process. I'd written poems about my daughter's struggle. All of them suffered from being made fun of when they spoke. Their English was not American. The younger ones could adapt quicker. But Oh, there were tons of problems they dealt with at school and church on a regular basis.

I thought they were not ready to start walking with the opposite sex. When was a good time? They were not invited to the sleepovers. All they had was each other. We did what we could to bolster them, like taking them sightseeing, but it was not enough. It was not enough in this culture.

I was involved in their schoolwork. I found some odd things in the library about places back home, which I knew firsthand. That pushed me into writing. But my children were hurting beyond words without our knowledge. I will come back to this before concluding this book. It has become the greatest trial of our lives. This has turned into sicknesses.

My husband was busy working with the company. We had the time of our lives. The children enjoyed the new scenery that unfolded before our eyes as we traveled about. Words can't describe the first Christmas in America, from dazzling lights to Christmas songs everywhere. But we missed the love of neighbors. That hurt. That really did hurt. That is not the end of the story. We kept going, and God is meeting our needs.

FINDING THE REAL ME

I just look back and see how the absence of excess stress can help unlock the ability to find your talents. You can think clearly. Jesus has taught us to guard against worry.

Life was more comfortable now. We could buy all we needed in one store without going round the city. With the washer, dryer, microwave, dishwasher, running water, stove, and other gadgets, living was simplified. The company provided us with maids, who came in to clean and help with laundry.

There was free time to watch the war that was going on in Iraq. Those were days of Desert Storm. That touched my being, and I found poetry coming out of me. One poem was published in the *San Ramon Valley Times*, on April 1, 1991. It was to the fallen soldier in the Gulf. My husband was very supportive of this. That is the good husband God gave me. My picture was put in the paper for free. This sparked outrage in some quarters of the Nigerian community in San Ramon. One man boldly voiced his anger. "The husband brought her here, and now she has her picture in the newspaper and not his." That exposed how some unbelieving husbands are. Thank God for peaceful Christian homes.

"He leadeth me beside the still waters. He restoreth my soul" (Ps. 23:2-3).

I had time for self-reflection. I started writing poetry. There were poetry reading centers near San Ramon. I went to read my poems there. That was how the newspaper found out about me. With time, the poems were many enough to make a small book entitled : *The Reflections of an African Poet*. My husband was very supportive of these ventures. I learned that quietness and confidence were my strengths. Whoever knew I was a poet? If we're relaxed, the real us can crawl out.

Gratitude flowed from my heart in songs. I bless God's throne with them. All songs do not have to be put on CDs. The Bible talks of singing a new song unto the Lord. We can do this. I may include some in this book. There are over fifty songs. I'm including a song I wrote at my kitchen table while I thought of my move to Los Angeles in August 1991, where I lived without my husband. This song could fit this season in which we live more. But there is the Lord's admonition to fear not.

Lord with Us Abide

Here we have no constant city
Lord with us abide
Hosts of hell are pressing harder
Lord with us abide
Here we wait and look for Jesus
For His word is our foundation
Thou wilt never fail nor falter
Lord with us abide

Jesus Lord the night is falling
Lord with us abide
Here the storms of life are raging
Lord with us abide
We remember Thy assurance
That you'll never live us helpless
Do not tarry Lord to help us
Lord with us abide.

Dark and fierce the closing chapters
Lord with us abide
Soon we'll see the chariots coming
Lord with us abide
As the days wane life is fiercer
And the hearts of men are failing
Lord remember all thy Promises
Lord with us abide.

—Victoria Udo

I saw calm beautiful streets in San Ramon, and I thought all of America was like this. How wrong I was. I'd seen Los Angeles on TV during the days of the Rodney King beating, so I couldn't flatter myself. At that time, I hadn't yet learned to drive the freeways, but God, our refuge and strength, was there. In a few years, my husband was called home by the parent company in Nigeria. My in-laws helped me find a job as a science teacher in a prestigious school in Pasadena, so I stayed back with the children in America. We had family and friends here, but I didn't know that the pace of life in America was so fast and structured. It could not compare with life from where we came.

My woes started when my British-trained principal could not stand seeing me with my five children. I was the only black woman on the staff of over fifty. There were two other African American brothers on staff, brilliant men. I didn't understand the principal's problem with me initially, because I tried my best to do my work to exceed expectations.

Many parents were impressed with the quality of my work. The favor was divine. There was a parent who asked me where I learned the science, I was teaching the children. She didn't imagine that there were universities in Africa, from where I came. In Africa, I had professors from around the globe as my teachers. I had my degrees in chemistry and mathematics. Not everybody does well with mathematical operations. There was a couple, the Dorios, a doctor, and his wife, who appreciated my work. Dr. Dorio accepted my invitation to come and speak with my eighth graders on how to choose their careers. His wife served in my classroom as a helper many times. The

Lord put help wherever help was needed. I still treasure a beautiful glass tray that David, their son, gave me for Christmas in 1992. I have owned it for twenty-nine years. This family served as strong support for me. There were other supportive families too. Sasha's mom and aunty were always there. This God has always been there for us. The Archibongs were there as guard rails in everything. I can't thank them enough. Without them, how could we have found Ribet Academy?

Behold the eye of the Lord is upon them that fear Him upon them that hope in His mercy.

There were a few teachers who understood the stress under which I worked. When I had to prepare the laboratory for teaching the next day, my children would wait with me till about eight at night. They asked how I was doing and that often gave me someone to share some practical issues with. You know there are some greetings that get more intimate replies than "fine, thank you." Some days I really needed encouragement, and God sent some through people and by reminding me of His Word. Nothing could replace the habit of having time alone with the Lord, and then praying as a family.

My children had their big challenges of not fitting in with the students in many ways, especially regarding their accent. Some of the students made fun of them and laughed at them. Some families take time to teach their children not to treat strangers unkindly. This was unheard of back home where we came from. The general philosophy is that you be very kind to strangers. The Caucasian children are very protected, because they are looked upon as strangers. My children had lost every status they had at home as Udo's children, their father being an accomplished geochemist. This is America, where you could become a millionaire selling popcorn. Many do worship heroes, and very few care for the quiet achiever who doesn't blow a trumpet.

Just after the fires that burnt Los Angeles, a beautiful grade school was erected from the ashes. After I'd finished teaching Sunday school one day, a ,friend Ruth, said, "Sis Vic can you come interview for the principalship of the new school? Her husband, Allister, was the director of this mission organization in Watts, Los Angeles. I was told it was a mission school. The Lord had made known to me something like that earlier in my life. I'm a product of a mission school owned by the Lutherans in Nigeria. Forms were filled out, and that weekend, the Lord worked so that my husband came into town from Nigeria on a company assignment. He filled in his part of the forms, and we submitted them. Without that, my forms could have been rejected as incomplete. The Americans, we found out later, abhor the concept of a husband and wife living separately because of work, except for military service. The interview was set for a week later.

Move Into Watts

*M*y mouth went dry as I sat before a board of twelve people, all white, to be interviewed for the post. So truly, are there mission fields in America? I asked myself. There are many mission fields in America. In our ignorance, we were taught that white people, in short, those in America and Europe, were all Christians. It's far from the truth. There was a time many people were Christians over here, but now the gods of materialism and sensualism have taken over. Thank God for the faithful remnant, and I believe you belong in this group.

I had left the affluent school in Pasadena, and I was moved to the Christian school near the housing projects. One late evening, we were moved into the top floor of the school, on Imperial Highway. It was a brand-new school, built at a cost of over a million dollars. It stood out beautifully in the neighborhood, for which I'm still very thankful. The children in this place may never have seen such a building, much less entered one. I was surprised to see that the single-family houses around the school were kind of small, but tall barbed-wire fences separated our school from some other tall buildings.

When night came, we prayed and slept. In the morning, I noticed that the neighborhood was different from the America I'd lived in a few days before. In my culture then, the working class lived in the housing, but not here. But there was no turning back at this point. It's for Jesus and the souls of the families, I told myself. This was the first major price I paid—the environment of the mission work. What was going to happen to my children? I could not have knowingly moved here.

The first thing that caught the attention of us all was the almost constant noise of sirens from ambulances. My second son, Nick, kept a count of the ambulances on a pad of paper. Some days, he could count nine. No one had told me there was a lot of gun violence around there. Let me quickly mention that God kept us from the bullets. He kept all the other missionaries and their families safe.

I was a mother with five children. We had put our hands on the plow. Could you compare this with the quiet, beautiful area of Chevron headquarters? What were we to do now? Nothing but pray for safety. Somebody had to go for the Lord. The children didn't know what danger the family was in, but I knew. My husband had gone back to his work in Lagos before this move. Was this part of divine guidance? Yes, it was.

The tests were about to start. We were soon visited by uninvited guests. About four huge men climbed the fence into our gated school property. They climbed upstairs to our apartment on the third floor and walked along the corridor, peeping into rooms that had no blinds at that time. But they never entered the rooms. Our Angels were on guard. We learned for the first time about gangs. It didn't matter, because God's will had to be done in that place.

I'd been trained by God in some other difficult terrain, which we won't talk about here. I see why lots of missionaries I read about growing up were single unmarried women. The men were often married. My heart was always wondering how our children felt. There were quite a few challenges. Did I bring my family into harm's way from the quiet lovely environment we had in San Ramon? But there is yet a city whose maker and builder is God. We are told, here we have no continuing city (Heb. 11:8–10).

"This is not what I thought it would be like," I would say to myself. My husband was far away across the ocean. Children were battling with acceptance from peers. Some had been wounded emotionally, and I could not tell. I learned that many of the children around there took drugs and smoked weed. God shielded my young children from it. I still can't identify these drugs thirty years after. These problems are the reasons the environment needed a missionary school. My children were all too old for the grade school we were starting in Watts.

I had to let the children go to the available schools in the neighborhood. Those were Los Angeles Christian School and Jordan High School. The Christian school was a great school. That was a great battle. The standards were not comparable to what we had known. But some good things came out of it. It was at Jordan High School that my daughter was picked as one of the one hundred students to represent Los Angeles County on a visit to the White

House. She went successfully. We will always remember that. I can't forget how shocked I was at the reaction of the community. In a two-thousand-student school, quite a number were in grades eleven and twelve. There was a college exhibition night, and only five parents came. I wept. I wondered what had happened to discourage them from being interested in schooling. I know more now. It was a hostile environment. It was poverty. It was years of deprivation.

God was faithful, and none of our children was killed. I learned new terms for survival. One of those terms is *jumped*. My second son, Nick, was jumped once on his way home from Jordan High. From our window on an upper floor, we could see many students beat him up. There was nothing we could do to help. He was wounded, but God spared his life. We were in Watts to save lives. How could we lose our son? I couldn't call the police. I came as an ambassador of Jesus Christ. Jesus had given His life for the redemption of mankind. But truly it was rough.

I remember the other missionaries who tried to speak up for our children. The greatest of the problems in this field, which I never expected, was lack of funds. We were not paid for about nine months, because we had not raised enough money to be paid from. For the first time in my adult life, I found that cultural ideals affected how we interpret Scripture. The school board chair had not yet been appointed. After he, a respected attorney from Orange County, came onto the board, things improved for us. But, prior to that, I couldn't just resign and leave. It was the longing of my heart to serve the King of Kings after that supernatural encounter with Heaven as an undergraduate.

Let the Work Begin

The school was a brand-new facility, as earlier stated. On the top floor, there was a wing dedicated to the mission office, where the director operated. They had young missionaries working on various aspects of outreach. There operated the Bible clubs, where various age groups came and were taught on their specific days. These were afterschool clubs. They were helped with homework. There was food collection and distribution to the community. An African was the director of this Watts work, working under the big bosses in Los Angeles. There were a lot of young whites working with him. But the headquarters was about ten miles away and controlled by the white brethren.

The school was another arm of this work, and there I was principal. Dear Sister Carol, a retired teacher was our first teacher. Oh, she was God sent. How knowledgeable and caring she was. We will talk more about her later. She went with me to Africa for summer training, and she was well loved. Mma Mbakara, the children called her. (The white madam)

As good practices dictate, we were on roll for one year before the school could begin. I was mentored by some godly principals for a time, to get me ready. But one thing was sure. I had a blueprint of our role as a school to reach out to the community. We operated as an evangelistic school. Other teachers were employed alongside me. They came from churches that supported them in finances. Our family was not yet funded, but it didn't matter. There was a sister Christian school of the same organization a few miles away, in Los Angeles. The principal (Bob) and his teachers did all they could to start us up and support us, but not financially. We proved God provides. Miraculously, He did provide for our financial needs. The mission headquarters had been resolute that we had to bring sponsors, otherwise we would not be paid. My husband had left a lot of money for us before going back to Nigeria. But after some time, the money ran out. There was a secret source from which God sent us funds for sustenance. It was a miracle.

I had a plan to help promote this school in the Watts community. Many in this community were skeptical. The mothers and grandmothers were chiefly the ones who responded to me. I had to go into the projects to tell them what a good and great opportunity it was that God had provided for them and their children. Where the dads were present, they just did their business and were not too involved. There was a particular family who lived by the projects who had been instrumental in securing the school in the neighborhood. That was the Shepherds family. Grandma was a fighter and a light in the community. God had put them there to encourage our family. They helped spread the word that we were there for the community's good. Can you blame the community for being suspicious of any new thing? Their stories were heartbreaking. But we were there with a solution. We wielded the weapon of prayer for the very foundations of the place. We invited men of God from Africa to work with us for the community.

I undertook a familiarization tour of the area, sitting on the well-kept lawns in front of their homes. I talked and talked with prayer. I shared the love of Jesus for them and all humans. Some willingly prayed and gave their hearts to Jesus. It's only the Lord who knows how seriously some took the exercise.

The responses were all different. The follow-up was largely the responsibility of the mission wing. The mothers were very receptive. I got used to the terrain quickly and prayed their children would pass the entrance examinations. It was not unusual to see grandmothers taking care of their grandchildren. Some of the mothers had taken off. God bless grandmothers everywhere who took up raising their grandchildren. Before the school opened, we had gathered a group of parents together to pray for the success of the school. We prayed for staff to be willing to come and for favor with the headquarters office on Twentieth Street. We were also required to attend Bible clubs on club days with the mission staff. Our children attended if they were available.

The backbone of the work of Watts Christian School was the prayer team we put together with the mothers. There were many reasons to celebrate God's answers to prayers. Sometimes the need was immediate, and we held hands in a circle and petitioned the Lord. We needed teachers from term to term. They needed to be certified and also financially prepared to raise funds. How many teachers of color, who would come out of college with huge student loan debts, could ever meet this requirement? The young white Christian girls from the Midwest were more available, but many could not stay past a year or two. We were ever more faced with threats of closure. At a point, it looked like I was the owner of the school, always pleading that the school not be closed down. My heart was touched by the needs of this community beyond expression. I'm told it's now just a community center. Hmm.

OPENING WITH KINDERGARTEN

The principal of our sister school, Bob, helped me with testing materials and Yvonne a certified kindergarten teacher for many years, married to the Shepard'sson. was able to complete the testing and do the orientation for the class with their parents. There were many blessings for these young children. The class size was small. All the baggage brought from home got slowly unpacked. Classroom language was getting the center place. The ones who needed help from the psychologist were being helped. The teacher and helper were doing excellent work.

Sometimes dear Sister Carol and I were almost knocking heads. I felt she needed to be more tolerant of Peter. She suggested that it would be better to let go of one child who was being too rowdy than to lose them all. Many times, the Lord would directly intervene. This beautiful morning, I was reading Leviticus 16:21–22 in my office. Teacher Carol brought up Peter and gave him an ultimatum. She wanted me to expel him, or she would quit. She was our only teacher for kindergarten. She sat across the desk from me.

We bowed our heads and prayed, then we asked Peter to recite the memory verse for the week. He innocently recited the verse. "But the goat on which the lot fell to be the scapegoat shall be presented alive before the Lord to make an atonement with him, and to let go for a scapegoat into the wilderness" (Lev. 16:10). We sat in silence, and Carol later stood up and left with him. The scapegoat of the world had atoned for Peter. We reminded ourselves, as we prayed with the student, that this was a mission school. Everything will not always be weighed on a scale. All of us would come up short, except for the scapegoat, our great Redeemer. That's why we were in South Central, to do the Master's bidding.

The children's mothers were also there at appointed times to help with various things. They exhibited lots of talents. They could decorate simple sandwiches to cause mouths to water. Their knitting skills produced fancy blankets for the cold winter months. They cooked delicious dishes for various occasions, like Jubilee, Black History Month, Christmas, and more. They were there to pray with me for school needs, which were not few.

Praying Alone

*M*any times, intense prayers were offered when I was alone with God. Early in the work, I had signed up to pray with an international team of intercessors, which my brother, Dr. Uduak Udofia, introduced me to. They had a conference venue in Long Beach, California. That was some nineteen miles from Watt's Christian School.

I signed up to pray between four and five in the morning. I went down to the school hall to pray. About thirty minutes into the prayers, I had a supernatural visitation. I may not be able to describe it in detail, but I'll try. A power like wind entered the hall with no windows. The entity began speaking, and I was told to write down what was said. It's in the heart of God for me to facilitate Christian education in Africa. The fruits of the schools will be receptacles for the fruits of the coming revival. I asked what the pattern was, and it was to be after the model of the Watts Christian School. It was a very intense time. Only heaven knows the things that transpired. I was deeply touched by them. One thing was certain—God was about to do some outstanding things. I felt scared but willing. I wrote these things down and later showed them to my husband when we met. But I was very excited and called the coordinator of prayers, not realizing it was only five.

He said, "Oh, Victoria, you could wait till morning?"

My husband responded, saying we should wait and see what God would do. I forgot about it for ten years. I did nothing to bring it to pass

I continued my work and kept wondering what was going to happen in the future, but I couldn't worry, because our lives were in God's hands. He never hurts us.

The richer schools in Orange County were willing to accommodate us on visits. Orange County had Christian schools that would willingly find time for us. Our students were mostly Hispanics and Blacks. Those other children played very cordially with our children. Never for once did those children pull back for any reason. It showed the world of children and I was happy to watch and learn. They hugged freely, and their teachers were kind. Surely there was a difference. These children showed that they were taught well, and it gave me hope. This was about twenty-five years ago. I hope we can still have this hope of a great America. Can I still thank God for Amy, Ebony, Asha, Edwina, Eka, Ubong, and the rest? We were family. These children are all grown now, and can provide for themselves, and sometimes for their parents now.

After the school opened formally, we continued our Bible studies and parenting classes weekly in the evenings, with the parents and interested community members. It was a fellowship time we all looked forward to. ACSI had given us articles that helped me in teaching the classes too. *Parenting God's Way*, by Gary Chapman, was also a great resource. Many parents confessed to being helped greatly. I was also benefited. Remember, I was a middle-aged mother at this time.

The ACSI had drummed into my psyche that the principal is the spiritual leader of the Christian school. Time spent alone with God was my power plug for daily success. There was no success for a project like this, unless every member of staff was carried along—from the janitor to the class assistant teachers. Whoever worked with the children must be Christian of a born-again persuasion. As should be expected of all human endeavors where any conglomeration of people works together, disagreements are bound to arise from time to time. In always striving to resolve these quickly and sincerely, we had the victory. We used the Matthew 18 principle. This point helped the staff to model the life of Jesus. It was a little problematic with the non-teaching staff. Some could not quickly latch onto the teachings. Remember, this was a mission, with God showing His redeeming power in the lives of former drug addicts and so on. God was still working on all of us, and so we had to patiently go along, knowing that God was able to fulfill His purpose. We kept our focus to raise disciples of Jesus in Watts who would raise others by and by.

A Strategy for Changing
Lives in Line with the Word

*T*his was a mission school, not just a Christian school. Sending a child to a Christian school is an indication that you want your child to be raised on Christian values. But there are some constraints that enable or disable that effort. There must be money. The fees are not cheap. But it's not enough to send the child to the available Christian schools. Apart from affordability, the most important thing is the interaction between the teacher and the child. So, it was my cardinal responsibility to inspire the workers with the mind of Christ. The teacher's heart must love the children and the Lord and have a vision for a successful academic life with a Christ-centered worldview. The school was evangelistic while also being about discipleship. Some establishments believe that God had finished reaching out to sinners and was now only consolidating the gains.

This work was also a startup for this community that had been characterized by oppression and violence for so long. I looked for every possible help to put a foundation of Godliness in place. Many Christian people gave the best they could to ensure the transformation of this community. The thing was, if you can't go in person, support with whatever your gifting is. Everybody can pray. A few of the ladies from Manhattan Beach and Orange County came to help the children read and do chapels. A lot of Bible memorization took place. As I went around to be mentored in Southern California, I found good programs that met our school's needs.

One such idea was building the life of the school around weekly themes. The following themes are still fresh in my mind, twenty-five years later.

- Paying Attention
- Punctuality
- Obedience
- Hard Work
- Gentleness
- Truthfulness
- Repentance
- Courage and Much More

The class teachers and helpers were diligent in tailoring lessons around the themes. I had my crown with the theme around it. I had a belt or shoulder strap. The teachers' assistants decorated the classrooms and corridors too. This went on from Monday to Friday and was adapted to the level of the young children. I hope those children, now adults, still remember and teach their children these things, if nothing else.

We had an intercessory team that included the director and his family, and that anchored the work. There were weekly nights of intercession. The fruits of this work had to abide, and it's only the Spirit that can do this. We had morning devotional times with the school children. We had a teacher's devotional session before the students arrived. It was a work bathed in prayer and the Word of God. We sang and marched and recited scriptures each day.

Our spirits had to be kept alive, because there were many uncertainties.

The school secretary had a heart of gold. She was very efficient in her duties. Her office and mine were kept up to date. She answered the questions of everyone with a smile. This school was a lighthouse in the community, and it had to be kept as such. There could be any type of inquiry from our headquarters office, and she knew what to say and do. Every worker made a major contribution toward raising the Watts Christian School. There was a rich young businessman at Long Beach who was a great supporter of this mission. He donated his car to our family, and we were grateful. A lot of the people who rallied around us in the field had noble hearts and pure motives. But that's all I can say here. We all had heard that God had a job He wanted to do to help poor families in South Central LA, and we had rallied to the call. The wife of this businessman and her sister were very committed to helping the inner city. I can't enumerate the things we went through, nor is it necessary. God, the judge, knew, took note, and it is okay. The bottom line is that families were reached, and some were saved. Children could attend classes in safety. How wonderful. No one ever shot a gun at us or the students. The community knew this was an important project for the future survival of their families. Let me share a vision I had one night while struggling with the work.

These Grow Only in the Valley

*A*n unspoken communication ensued. What if no one had cared to educate her, then all her chances could have vanished into thin air. A very beautiful vision had come to my mind now, and there were many. This came to me while serving in Watts Christian School.

He sends messages in various ways, even in dreams and visions, as He chooses. But it's always in alignment with His Word.

One night, I saw a girl of about five years, with torn clothes on her back, in a very destitute condition. As I turned to pay closer attention. I was shown that someone had been kind enough and patient enough to put her through school. She had cooperated and succeeded in school. It was quite uplifting to learn from the scenes that followed in the vision.

I saw a vendor carrying magazines with this once destitute girl's picture on the front page. She was twenty-one then and so beautiful.

There have been many. I pondered on the happenings then continued my journey down a steep, unpaved road. It brought to my mind some of the unpaved paths up and down some hills where I grew up in Ndiya. Some effort was needed to navigate it safely. At last, I arrived at the bottom of the hill, and who can guess what I saw? I remember to this day that it was a bush of lush, shiny green leaves. They had serrated edges lined with white. Never had I seen a plant like this on the earth. It grew beautiful white blossoms with an invigorating scent never known before. I was so happy and amazed. Very excitedly, I bent over to pluck it.

Then a commanding voice spoke to me. "Do not pluck these! They are meant for wayworn travelers who pass this way. They only grow in the valley." I was shocked to hear the voice, but I learned my lesson.

I inhaled some of its scent and felt refreshed, then I continued on my journey upward. Who did not need such refreshing in the vineyard of Watts? I climbed onward. The sun's rays fell on the side of the hill, and its shadow was on the other side. Then I awoke. I felt encouraged.

Even though I walk through the valley of the shadow of death I fear no evil for thou art with me.

I will even make a way in the wilderness and rivers in the desert, I give waters in the wilderness and rivers in the desert to give drink to my people my chosen. Isaiah 43:19b–20b.

Is it possible that there are times when we walk through these dark valleys without knowing? But the Lord, who knows our needs, does provide encouragement. The Bible does confirm it.

This is how the Eternal chooses to walk with me. I never get intimidated by men. I respect men, but I bow before Him, the Judge of the whole earth. When I awoke, I drew fresh strength from the Word. He who helped us can help any other who cry out to Him and will help in the future.

> "Hast thou not known? hast thou not heard, that the everlasting God, the Lord, the Creator of the ends of the earth, fainteth not, neither is weary? there is no searching of his understanding. He giveth power to the faint, and to them that have no might he increaseth strength. Even the youths shall faint and be weary, and the young men shall utterly fall: But they that wait upon the Lord shall renew their strength; they shall mount up with wings as eagles; they shall run, and not be weary, and they shall walk, and not faint" (Isa. 40:28–31).

I am persuaded that whatever responsibility God gives even the least of His children He will sustain them in the challenges. We don't see Him but we see His handwork.

THE LATER YEARS IN THE WATTS SCHOOL

*A*s the first two years were coming to a close, the children were in second grade, and more students had been admitted. Our little community was growing. My adaptation to the culture was growing. Let me narrate another incident that happened as I was learning to adapt. One of the beautiful ladies who drove every day from her home in Manhattan Beach to teach told us a story during our staff prayer time.

She requested prayer for her cat, that had just had surgery costing $2,000. I couldn't imagine that such an amount was spent on an animal while we barely had enough to eat. But that cat was her family, and she was not responsible for us, I reasoned. Remember, we were new to the culture.

My timeline of development was inspired by Principal Mary, of Orange County, who had taught me many things and answered my questions. There was an advertisement for training from a group affiliated with the Association of Christin Schools International. I needed to go. The mission gave permission and paid my fare. I had to call the organizers in Colorado Springs to explain my situation. I had no money for hotel or conference fees. The secretary of the conference told me to call back the next day. I later learned that was to give her time to discuss it with her husband. She had never seen me.

I called back the next day and was pleasantly surprised by the Lord. The secretary told me I was allowed to come to the conference without paying the conference fees. She gave me their address. She told me to look under a big stone in front of their house on arrival. I was to take the key and open the door, leave my box, and go to join them at the conference. I was happy that Christianity, the old-fashioned way, still worked. She heard I had an accent. I was in Watts. I found out her husband was the president of a well-known Christian university. Faith works. Yes, it still works! I had to be brave and take a rental car from the airport to their house and the conference venue at the DoubleTree Hotel. The missionary to Watts also needed courage, which the Lord supplied. It was time for some refreshing.

I needed to be there at the conference. I learned so much that helped me to run the school. Some serious discussions arose, and contributions were called for. I raised my hand and said something. I think there were about a thousand administrators of Christian schools there, and I could only count six principals of color. My suggestion was that young black children needed scholarships to attend Christian schools. Education is a costly venture, and those whose hearts the Lord has touched can encourage the young black talents, otherwise the disparity will be too much in the future. Many of the children we met in Watts had no dads living with them. The Lord helped many of those grandmas do great work with those grandchildren (Prov. 22:6). The children are now all grown. Succeeding generations will continue until Jesus returns. Let us continue to work each day. God will repay.

Train up a child in the way he should go: and when he is old, he will not depart from it.

Children of all colors need training. We had a document: "The Christian Philosophy of Education," which helped me greatly to forge a direction for the school. The training had this document as foundational. All children, men, and women are equally precious. No one determined his or her birth parents or birthplace. Everybody has a gift with which to bless the world if nurtured in a good environment. The sinful nature is inherent in all from birth, but Jesus came to save us all. Children who have been raised for the Lord may stray from the path at some point in time. But they will return, as we continue to pray. This is why Christian education is important. It has been a great privilege to touch the lives of those made in God's image.

What is there to be done in missions in America's inner cities? From my standpoint, I say:

Bringing hope to the families.
Love the people, who are fellow Americans like us all.
Give the young, especially, a sense of belonging in this nation.
Encourage the escape from the circle of violence and poverty.

Help connect them to abundant resources of this land.
The most lasting one is sharing Jesus the Savior with them.
There are a few experiences I can share.

There were opportunities to go inside the projects to share the love of Jesus. A lot of the homes had smoke whenever I visited, but there were some free of smoke. That was very encouraging. I could sit and talk. Some of the ladies and men had skills that could be used productively.

There was a time I'd asked the men to draw. Oh, what great artists I found. If we had encouragement, those men could have ended up on the front stage. I still wonder at how talents like that get wasted without support. The apathy and mistrust there did not help things. The people had stories of past experiences.

On my part, there was fear sometimes when a strong, angry-looking man was approaching, especially along the alleys. But I dared not express it. Whom would I tell? My husband was thousands of miles away, across the Atlantic. Other family members in the US were busy with their lives. No one sent me here but the Lord. Remember, I had my five children. The eldest was college age. But I had to be strong when I saw the people we had come to rescue.

Poor Peter's mom had nine kids with eight men. We had Peter in our mission school. This mother was young, like in her early thirties. She braided hair to augment her social security check. She was always braiding and had no time to come to answer school questions. She was a single mother. What a burden she carried. I had to go and talk to her about her son in her home in the projects. That was the only way out.

How was I expected to handle child abuse cases? Some children came with visible marks on their bodies. On one such occasion, the second-grade teacher went ahead with the report to the Child Protective Agency. A lot of debate went into such things.

Three years passed, and then, during the fourth, I had a stroke. In the words of the Italian doctor who handled my case, "Were you trying to kill yourself? You are a mother of five. In America being a mother of one is enough work. You are a full-time missionary living among the people. You are doing a master's in education. This is way too much."

True it was too much for this mortal body. Indeed, it was. Yes, I still remember having dinner with my son Nsi, who had come from the university that evening to check on us. We prayed and thanked the Lord for His goodness Nsikak was around. We retired to our rooms for the night. Early the next morning, I tried to go to the bathroom and fell to the ground. This happened three times. I just lay there until my daughter Udy came for morning prayers. I told her my condition, and she summoned the older siblings, for the family was united in this mission. My husband was working for Chevron in Nigeria at this time. Earlier, we had appealed to Chevron to please transfer my husband to their nearby office in South California to keep the family together. They could not. Nigeria was responsible for such decision.

We also hold no one responsible for our fate. It was a stroke. I thought I was going to appear before my Maker immediately. Then

I tried signing some checks so the family could keep alive till Dad came. My hand could not write on the paper. God knew ahead of time and brought my son from college that evening. I never suspected I was sick. I was taken to Downey Memorial Hospital. I learned to walk again. The Lord was there in every way.

It's been more than twenty years since then, and I'm still here. The Lord is my shepherd and the shepherd of all who trust in Him. That was what caused my husband to finally quit his well-paying job. The mission organization had wanted him to quit his job and join the family here, but there was no promise of funds to sustain our family. However, in 1997, we were all in South-Central Los Angeles. My husband had decided he would serve in the mission until retirement. He came on board and took over the administration of the school gradually. We are grateful that God looked out for the small school, but things didn't go as we planned in some areas. God saw the future.

The issue of raising funds to get paid was still there. Some of our people who knew what kind of job OT had given up to come and serve in Watts were very angry. But we owe our all to the Lord, and each person will appear before him at last. After a time, my husband sent me home to Nigeria to rest. When I was well, I joined the work again.

Our children went through very trying situations in their lives. The discrimination they experienced in school here in America would take a whole new book to tell. This was having a terrible adverse effect on their lives, which I did not see.

The day came for the graduation of the fifth graders who had started at the school as kindergarteners. It was a beautiful day. It was a mission accomplished. God had many witnesses that day. The stories of the struggle of the people and the rise of the school were told. Our pastor was there for the first time, and he loved what he saw and heard.

Because our family served there, good things came to many families in the area. Those children could go to school in relative safety. Many of God's people joined hands to pull those little ones through to safety. Attorney Letterman and his wife, Mary, were used to fighting for us. Many white brethren from the richer areas stood up and made their voices heard, as did some of the others of color. The Shephards, who bought the land and helped as voices for the community, deserve special mention. Brother and Sister Nzegwu, the directors of World Impact Watts, gave their all. We raised our children together, but all their children were born here.

When last I checked, many of those students had gone on to Christian Colleges and are on track with their lives. There are still mission fields in America today. Seriously, there are many, many mission fields ready for harvest. You don't have to go overseas to be a missionary. God led us on. At this point in the journey, God had proved over and over that He still does the impossible.

THROUGH THE VALLEY OF DARK SHADOWS

*I*t looked like the Udo family lost all because of our choice to go and serve in Watts. No, never! When World Impact asked us to leave suddenly because we could not raise funds, we were stranded, but it was temporarily. Then they asked the Nzegwu family to leave—a family of eight without accommodation, stranded. But today, those children have been situated by the Lord. Allister Nzegwu directed the construction of the Watts School under the mission with all integrity. When we had no accommodation or money to fall back on after being forced out, God provided help. That is after we were told to leave the work in Watts. So many suggested litigations, but how could we? The Lord said we could not go to court in this matter, for they are brethren. After praying and waiting on the Lord, C. Ikonte, a brother in the Lord, who took to my husband during one of our outreaches, offered to cosign for an apartment with my husband in West Covina. That was a lifesaver, because the mission deadline was upon us. We were given two weeks to move.

We went about looking at houses with our family, but we were told no one would sell us a house because we had no credit. It proved to be one of the valleys along our pathway We found a place. Though the place looked okay, I had my fears because of how closely the families lived. What were we going to use to sustain the family? We had to turn to the state for Social Security. My husband searched for jobs for a long time in the Los Angeles area but found nothing. The mission pulled the scholarship they'd given my daughter, and her world collapsed. She was a student at BIOLA University. Someone alerted my husband, and when he arrived, he didn't like what he saw.

One of our sons had a breakdown on a mission trip to Mexicali with our church youth group, and my husband had to come in from overseas to care for him. My brother in Arizona and his wife took him to their home for a time. The family had rallied around us, and it was a near tragedy. The children didn't seem to be able to handle the stress of the journey.

I can do a little chronicle here in order. My son had a breakdown in 1994 when we were all in an affluent school. I rallied our praying friends here and overseas. The university hospital did its best. Then I moved to Watts, and my son had to attend a new school when he got well. I had a stroke in 1997 in Watts, which caused my husband to leave his million-naira job and come to Watts. In 1997, we were ejected from Watts. We were on the road on the night of 2000. The world was not sure what was going to happen, but we're still here, twenty years after.

We were forced to move from West Covina to Eagle Rock because of an unforeseen situation. People did not know our struggles.

"Eye hath not seen, nor ear heard...the things which
God hath prepared for them that love Him" (1 Cor.
2:5 and 9).

No one needed to pay the price for our discipleship. The Lord had united our hearts as one. Not one day did my husband say, "You are the cause of this suffering." I had to bear my cross, a heavy one, and he did too.

The health of our children was deteriorating. Here we were, advocates for the young. But God did not say that if we served Him there wouldn't be problems. He is still Lord. We have prayed and prayed. Families have joined us for twenty-one-day fasts. We can't tell it all. This is the family that prevailers were sent to in Calabar, and they prevailed. We have not reached the end, so we're still looking up. We're still mortals on a journey. Men looked at us with ordinary eyes, but we knew who had called us.

My husband secured a position as a lecturer at Santa Monica College during our sojourn in West Covina. But soon the position was no more. He was the last to come and first to go.

An Oasis in the Desert

We did substitute teaching and suffered some humiliation from friends and foes. Though my husband had a PhD in petroleum geochemistry, he humbled himself and went back to school for a teacher credential in America. God was still there in Eagle Rock. We drove the two boys to school every day, while also doing our substitute teaching. We drove about twenty miles each morning to our schools. The children all had to attend their schools—junior high and senior high. The children had their weekly sports to attend, depending on their season. The basketball season was a highlight.

But one of the boys had a meltdown at a citywide prayer meeting. He ran out with the Bible shouting. He was about fourteen. We were in for another battle. He was taken to the hospital, and that went on and on. The burden was getting heavier by the day. But God kept people who helped us everywhere we went. We prayed with friends too.

The house rent was a battle. The landlord, who was a brother in our church congregation, let us off in two months after we paid what we could. Finally, God helped us to pay for it all. You know when people label you, anything can be said. We paid that money when we started a regular job. God always makes a way, where there is no way.

One of those hard days, as I was bringing back one of my sons from the clinic, I met a Nigerian on the bus. We talked about Jesus. I found out he was going to a Christian group about ten minutes from our home. These were days when we had no help in prayers. We were not allowed to take our son to church because of his disorientation. And we couldn't leave him alone at home. We needed to be with him always.

We got connected with praying people, and God did great things. He leads.

I went with him and met Pastor Barajas of Victory Outreach. They had a prayer room that had soft Christian music going on all the time. This was a great relief for me. God provided sisters who prayed earnestly. We prayed, and God answered prayers. Oh, beautiful prayer times. This group was on the cutting edge of evangelism. Young people who had been delivered from addiction to drugs and gangs were vibrant, serving the Lord. All along our journey, God provided shelters and resting places for refreshing. This was one of those. God has given us reasons to celebrate.

God has also given us Reasons to Celebrate

I come from a very warm, people-friendly background. This God gave us opportunities to celebrate, not only to work. We also celebrated in the church with the brethren when we celebrated my husband's fiftieth birthday. Fifty sounded so big. The whole Akwa Ibom community in the Los Angeles area was there. Then we celebrated his seventieth here in Bakersfield. Our Akwa Ibom community attended. Some teachers from Golden Valley High were there too. Some brethren from Tehachapi, including our pastor, came. But we were so very grateful to our friend and sister who traveled from Doylestown, in Philadelphia, to attend.

Her husband, Yinka, released her for a week to be here and help. Our friendship dates back about fifty years, from Ife University, Iyabo, and Yinka Williams. Iyabo has encouraged me through prayers to write this book. They moved to the west coast recently to be nearer their grandchildren, and I'm thankful too, because we're now closer. God knows we need friends and family. He said in the beginning, "It is not good for man to be alone."

In Bakersfield, He provided a job as soon as we arrived. He gave us students to disciple.

My husband had a teaching credential in Nigeria, before switching to geochemistry, which he studied in Julich, Germany. He talked about our moving to Bakersfield. Etekamba had left the oil company some years earlier and was working in the Los Angeles area. There was all sorts of uncertainty, no permanent work, no secure accommodation. God led us to move to Bakersfield, where my eldest brother-in-law lived.

I had a serious objection in my heart to moving. That led to seriously seeking God's face in prayer. He gave me a word I could hold on to. He promised to spread a table before us in Bakersfield. I could share this with the family, and we could pray into it. My husband had already fixed his heart to move to Bakersfield.

Let me point out that God did something in Bakersfield to show that He led us. You remember that my husband left his million-naira oil company job because of the family. Many thought he had done the worst thing in life.

"God is not a man that He should lie" (Num. 23:19).

At the first school he went to substitute for chemistry, he got hired for a permanent position. This is how it started. He saw a lady rolling an audio-visual set, which seemed a little too much for her, so he stretched out his hand to steady the cart. From there they started talking, and she came into his classroom. He had gone in early and set his class, which impressed the lady. She spoke with him and found he was a seasoned teacher. She asked if he would like a full-time position. This was a lady with authority, but my husband never knew. He was just being himself when he decided to help with the cart.

You know the weapons of our warfare are not carnal. Do you know your gentle smile, your polite answers, could be part of your weaponry? He said yes to her question. He was teaching and working on his credential. The district formalized his appointment after he completed his credentials. He became a tenant in his brother's house, never owing him rent. The home was just six minutes from work.

After fourteen years, God gave us our own retirement home. Okon taught at Golden Valley High School for fifteen years. Christian students were meeting in his classroom, where he served as patron. Is this not a beautiful Savior? Many lives were touched for the Lord. Was the mission call over? No!

I continued as a substitute teacher in America so I could be available for God's other assignments. When last I checked my passport, I'd traveled over thirty times to and from Africa. He who pairs people up knew who I had to marry to be fit for His plan, and my husband was fit for his own. He serves as an assistant pastor in our church in Tehachapi. God is King. God sent me back for some years to start a Christian school in my State, Akwa Ibom, Nigeria. You may hear of it in a new book. I was a missionary to my people, but I will share a little peradventure I can't write again. I will be seventy by the time you read this book.

Birth of Redemption Academy

In 2004, my husband and I went with the rest of the larger family to bury my mother-in-law, Mma Atim. After the ceremony, it was time to come back to the US. As we were packing, members of the Nigeria Christian Graduate Executive came to where we were lodging. We exchanged pleasantries, and then they let us know why they'd come.

They requested of my husband that he permit me to come to give an orientation lecture on the running of the Christian school they were intending to open in September. This was April. My husband conceded, and we continued chatting. I asked a few questions about their school team. They had not put anything in that direction in place. I went into the room to get some snacks for them, and what I heard on my return shocked me. They had a second request now.

They said to my husband, Dr. Udo, can you please allow your wife to come and spend three months getting the school started. I sat speechless, looking at my husband. In his gentle way, he bent over to me and said, "Eno, maybe this is what God was talking about ten years ago?"

I broke down in tears. Lord, how could I part from this man again after all the days of his schooling and our living apart? I had lived here for fifteen years and gotten used to the American ways. God, who moves in steady and planned ways, had already gotten my heart ten years before now. He is Sovereign. I still bow before Him as I recount this.

That team led by Justice Ita Mbaba took us to the site of the school at Obio Etoi village .It took more than a mile of dirt road with potholes from the broken down tarred road. My heart was still heavy. Another miracle happened. We saw Mr Peter Ikpe, an old friend at Calabar driving up in his car. The team stopped and what hearty greetings ensued. His house was opposite this school's site.

I was comforted. Should I have any problem with the villagers, I could run to his family. God had gone ahead of me, the God I know.

Since 1994, when He gave me the concept of life bridges, I've been going to Africa on summer holidays to share what I learned from ACSI with Christian schools and groups. The whole purpose in Christian Education is to give children a firm foundation in the Lord to guide them in life. The work turned into three years, with provision for frequent visits to my family. That school is Redemption Academy, which is flourishing today. God raised Lynda to take the work from me. I still peep in when I can. For me, the most important aspect is to help students create truly Christ-centered world views.

When I talk of a Christ-centered worldview, I want to remind us what that means.

- God is the Creator and sustainer of the universe. He created all mankind in His image, and all life emanates from Him. Because of this, all men deserve to be treated with respect. This is the foundation for fairness in the treatment of other men.

This was a huge change for me, coming from a background where we still had servants in the home. I learned to value people everywhere. This seemed to put me in trouble, because some of our ladies back home in Nigeria still have the thick line between our children and the hired servants. The lens of Christian education is revealing.

- Man is a fallen being and incapable of satisfying the righteous demands of a holy God.

  This means that when you deal with the unsaved, you should not expect standards of rightousness, which only the saved can attain, no matter the age. Only the regenerated man is capable of living above the world.

- Jesus is the Redeemer who died and shed His blood that our sins may be forgiven. This means we should find every opportunity to share the Gospel for the salvation of the soul. Good works alone will not suffice.

  Every family should lay this foundation in their children. Wherever there is the Lord's saving grace, the fruit of righteousness will shine through. I will come back to this work in Nigeria.

God raised various individuals and organizations to help me in facilitating the establishment of Christian schools in Nigeria. Ntiense and Anietie Ubon-Israel were my first host and hostess when I would arrive Lagos from the USA not ten times. Annie as she is fondly called hosted scores of guests at no cost, joggling us between rooms. We ate and drank and I don't know if we remembered to leave gifts to help continue such hospitality. I always met prayer teams and was fortunate to pray those Kingdom prayers. The

Lord met me there many times. This work took prayers for there were many adversaries.

Many Christian schools were blessed, from Lagos to Abuja and the East. My State of birth, Akwa Ibom, had their share of the blessing too. The heart of the matter is developing the mind of Christ. My prayer is that God will raise faithful men and women who will raise others. My brother Dr Uduak Udofia caught onto the vision right from my first presentation with his friends James Essien and Joshua Israel May God bless the faithful teachers who are learning along with us. Imaobong Joseph, Eno Inyangetuk, Florence Mba, Nseobong Ukut, Ufeli Awomukwu and Nyong received the impartation to work with their whole heart as the pioneer teachers.Victor Etienam joined the staff a little later. The city knew that something new had come to Akwa Ibom.The school set a standard of no cheating during exams. Excellence and hardwork took the center stage. Lynda Ekpenyong who took over Redemption Academy did her best. What can I say of Abasifreke, my faithful helper who died as I was leaving for Botswana? Mrs Iquo Udo was there by me for all I needed during those trying days. My brother Uduak and his wife Ekom were my main host family at home and they gave me the best.

There were threats of armed robbers during some land trips. God raised prayer teams with Sister Comfort Essien as coordinator. Ekwere life Bridges was hand picked by God for this work. You may not be able to pronounce these names but say a prayer that we may be faithful till God calls us home. During those pioneering years we knew when we went to work and not when we closed each day.

The pioneer students aka the Kings have their stories of healing, provision, compassion and enabling. Utomobong was the first student to arrive. Godly teachers rallied around Ekopema Inyang and changed his story for good. Sickness bowed to Jesus in the life of Emmanuel Johnny. He was able to represent Nigeria in Europe in Informatics, and came first, because Redemption Academy had a computer laboratory in her second year. God met every need. Mr. John Udo the registrar of the University of Uyo was our school Board chairman for many years. Prof Ashong Ashong and late Dr. Itina were loyal pioneer Board members. Mike Udoh served with all his heart. Members of NCGF served with a passion. God awoke the team to work. It is a successful endeavor, giving glory to God.

A New Daughter

The Lord guides and leads in unexpected ways for our good. He had assured me of preparing a table for us in Bakersfield, which is where we live. Do you have a personal promise from the Lord? Hold on to it. If God said it, He will do it.

We are getting older, and the body is getting a bit feeble. I continued substitute teaching in Bakersfield. It helped me to reach out to the students. One day, I called my doctor's office from school during a math class. The doctor's assistant immediately called an ambulance to come and take me to the hospital. I tried to argue that it was not a heart attack, but she did not listen. Can you imagine my embarrassment when the ambulance drove into the school? But I appreciate her concern for my life. Remember, my husband works here permanently. How permanent? The ninth graders were excited. But the doctors at the hospital only saw a pinched nerve, after dozens of tests.

The next morning, the emergency room physician offered to send a doctor who was from Nigeria to come and take care of me.

He asked if that was okay with me. I said yes. Never did I know that God was about to fill up my Bakersfield table. The brilliant, beautiful young doctor, whom I call Ebun in this book, came in with a smile. I was reading my Word. She sat by me, and we started talking. We didn't understand each other's native languages. As we talked about my condition, she suddenly said to me, "Mma, please, would you be my mother in Bakersfield?" I very readily said yes. I said to myself, "Did I hear her well?" Yes, I did, and God sent her.

We have had a mother–daughter relationship. Her husband is now part of the ring, and her children call me Grandma. They all relate happily with us in the family. Her husband is Nsi's age too. Let me remind you that Nsi is my firstborn. God knew I needed a doctor for a daughter.

I could tell you so much more about this relationship. My husband was very sick after his abdominal surgery. He was operated upon twice. The Covid epidemic had already started. One evening, Ebun came in her hospital gown and asked to see my husband. She was coming directly from work. The Covid pandemic was here already. She had never come in her work clothes. She did not sit. Etekamba could barely walk, and when she saw him and listened to him, she asked us to call the ambulance immediately. She called the hospital too. That was how my husband was saved from a distended abdomen. I may not remember the real name. Nsi and their family moved to Sacramento because of work. They still visit, but God sent us other children. God showed up again for us.

THAT IS THE GOD I KNOW. HE LEADS ALONG LIFE'S JOURNEY.

We had to drive forty-five minutes each way to church in our little hill city of Tehachapi. We could see snow in its season. The windy roads presented quite a challenge for me. My husband did most of the driving. I was not impressed, initially, to say the least, with the congregation. In spite of the care the pastor showed, the numbers were dwindling. But when I saw the love and care Pastor showed the flock, I knew God had yet something great to teach me. His care for handicapped members surpasses explanation. Our pastor spent time designing Bible study guides and prayer pamphlets. Those resources bless men everywhere, including in our native Africa. The Spirit focused me on the thing I'd never seen in the same manner anywhere else—the love of the saints.

When we moved into our present home, it was a miracle. Everyone said no one would give us a loan at this stage, but God did. God did it to show that He is Sovereign. After we came back from a camp meeting in July 2019, I developed tendonitis, which did not let me go to work for more than eight months. We needed to buy a house, and in spite of my not working, we still bought a beautiful house. God went before us. It appeared that since he left the Chevron job, life would be terrible. The day we moved was a real spectacle. The pastor drove the moving truck. All the able-bodied men rallied to the task. The ladies were not left behind. The pastor and his wife bought new bedding and prepared the guest room for me. I was brought in there while the ladies put things in place. I could not do a thing. My husband went for the pizza to give to the work team. The beauty was that they are all white brethren. Blessed be the name of the Lord. So three weeks passed since I started work again and the Covid situation befell the country. But since I'd worked three weeks before schools closed, I had a pay stub to show and qualify for Covid unemployment. Are you seeing the hand of the Lord? God is good.

Just like in Christian schools, when the leader of the team sets an example, it affects the whole team. Pastor Mark Staller leads us to share about our week very openly. We could pray with knowledge for each other. We share meals besides praying together. It has become a very warm group. I became close with another sister. She would come to help me with the house arrangement. It was okay for her to enter everywhere. Her husband was the superintendent of schools for a time. But there was no vanity about her. Brenda was very good at flower arrangements and repairs during my husband's seventieth birthday celebration I am sure she will help with mine She was always ready to help. Sylvia, the pastor's wife, was a jewel. She was always giving, and she led the women in Bible studies. Having now walked with the Lord for these fifty years, I recognized things that are authentic. The pastor treats my husband as an older brother. The openness we share is a treasure. There is a friendship. God satisfies. It's difficult to get assimilated into a new culture, but with God, it's easier. It took God alone to bring us to this point.

About ten years ago, we hosted friends and relations in Tehachapi, at the pastor's house. Our son, Nsi, was receiving his wife from India. We went with him for his marriage to Sunaina Dar, in India. It was a happy, one-week trip. Sunaina's family and church family shared the love of God with us. We celebrated and were happy. Friends traveled for up to three hours to come, and we were happy. The Tehachapi church family loved our son and his wife. They prayed with them for about eight years before they had their baby. They are still beloved, though they moved away for work.

For the first time, I had church family praying for my trips and openly giving for the needs of the school outreaches overseas This is quite outstanding. We had a loving church family in Los Angeles too, with dear Pastor Elmer and Sister Helen. They loved us and cared. I still remember dear Elmer carrying a refrigerator with Brother Jack up our stairs to help us. Sister Helen typed out my original songs and got Sister Amy, of the Medford church, to listen to my taped voice and transcribe it into staff notation. Brother Jensen worked with the children on their instruments. Brother Ron faithfully mentored the boys. How could I forget Pastor Bill, sitting with my mother outside the theater during my surgery for hours? Mother could have fainted alone, had he not been there, not knowing why it took me so long to wake from the anesthesia. God sent the Etims, who were our friends from Uyo, to the Los Angeles church. I baked their wedding cake years ago. That is just trying to be flippant. But what I talk about is our hilltop church and the partnership in school outreach to Africa and daily living. That is the call the Lord gave me, and that is what satisfies my soul.

Growing up, we had some dreams, but God had purposes for our lives. What's important is to stand on God's Word and follow Him humbly. At the end of our lives, we will stand before our Savior. It's a privilege to be saved and to be given anything to do in His name. I love Jesus, who first loved me. There have been challenges, but none is greater at overcoming them than our Savior. We are unprofitable servants at best. My husband funded those trips home, with the help of the Almighty. Even my dentist is a Christian, and she sends gifts when I travel home on mission trips. When we remember all the divine interventions and victories, we give all the glory to God our Savior. You can see that it's been a simple daily walk, but God shows up daily. Many people consider success to be the ability to buy a big house, have educated children, drive nice cars, and accumulate other gadgets. We know these things make life, easier but the Word shows the true path to success .I did not go looking for a Christian dentist. God graciously leads me to these Christian professionals.

One day I bought some medication to use for my toe nail fungus. I did not know that the lady behind me was a doctor. She followed me outside and told me how that medication hurt her patient. She told me not to use it. Does God care to the least things about us.

Maybe this last piece will answer the questions of some young hearts. In the university during our youthful days, it was very important to be sure of who your life partner was going to be. I was the firstborn child in our home, and some characteristics come with the birth order, from our studies and observation. I'm a bit independent and bold. God uses these traits when He wants. I was also looking forward to marrying a man with these traits and more. But my husband appeared too quiet and withdrawn. But he is a committed lover

When I was working back in Africa the temptations that upset me were many. Our fellow teachers would come in with expensive clothes to show what their husbands had bought for them. For our family, the comfortable thing was that I did the shopping for everyone. My husband gave approval for me to spend the money. If I ever did any wasteful spending, would that not be hurting me? Why did the teachers need to bring those in? I don't know. But Jesus is the solid rock. Whoever builds on Him is secure from storms. The same gentle dependable character shows forth in church, at work, and so on.

This must have been the reason one of his principals in Golden Valley went to His classroom to tell him something very important. That was when the government was giving out pink slips to teachers a few years ago. He said, "Dr. Udo, I have come to tell you that you will not be receiving the pink slip." That was to show you were laid off. It was unheard of that the head of a school would go to inform a teacher he was not going to be given the pink slip.

As we begin to age, the wisdom of God shines forth more and more, and we see His resplendent beauty. My husband has a gift of service. He also has God-given wisdom, which has brought solutions on many occasions. He takes care of me in ways that confound me. I lack words to use and thank him. He waits for us to finish eating, and as soon as I start to clear the dishes, he says, "Leave them there. You've been on your feet cooking." The big King's bed is a challenge for me, and he says, "I got it."

I don't remember when last I vacuumed the house. I can go on and on, and it may annoy some people. But this is the pearl God gave me and I did not realize it at first. I thought I needed a man who could talk sweet all the time. You should have seen him putting my things together for any of my mission trips when he was still teaching. If I ever called from Africa to say that any of my supplies were running low, he would send DHL as soon as possible. This is the God of infinite wisdom, who knows all men and all situations ahead of time.

In Conclusion

God has led us, and I praise His name. He has led countless saints. There is deep trust and peace in following Him.

God can be trusted. He will always come through but not on our terms. He knows best. The most important thing in life is to set our priorities, as God gives us breath according to His Word. Whatever men may say, you have seen from these accounts that there is God! You need to listen to Him through His word, the Bible and follow Him. We need to pass on the baton of truth and faith to the next generation. The place to train the children is around the simple interactive family altar. We read the Word, discuss, let the children speak their minds, and learn together. Nothing is greater than a good example. There is no reset in life. God is reaching out to us in love. Let us take hold of His outstretched Hand with the nail prints.

Besides the focus on our families, the God I know is the Lord of Hosts. He is surrounded by hosts of angels and is Lord of countless saints. He deserves our worship. We can sing, we can read scriptures aloud, we can praise Him. As I flee from the wrath to come in repentance, I invite you to join me. Awake in your inner man and endeavor to be intimate with the God of Heaven and earth, the King of Kings and Lord of Lords. He deserves all adoration not just listening to others singing. Let us beef up His praise, He is worthy. Have your praise corner. If you spend a prolonged time in His presence, you will be surprised by a refreshing you have never experienced. You can use your Bible to help you praise the Lord. The psalms can be read and expounded upon. Meditate on the Scripture and enrich your praise. He who comes to God must believe that He is, and that He is a rewarder of them that diligently seek Him. Join to walk besides the still waters no matter the noise around. You will be happy you did. Jesus says of Himself. In Revelation 1:18 "I am he that liveth and was dead and behold I am alive for evermore Amen and have the keys of hell and of death." Hallelujah! What more?

CPSIA information can be obtained
at www.ICGtesting.com
Printed in the USA
FSHW020648030921

9 781662 816765